# HEARTF♥LL D♥GS

### Melanie (Mellie) Test

MagicWithMellie.com

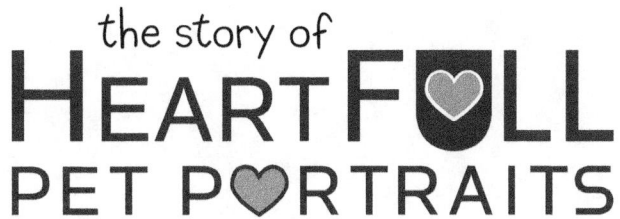

the story of
# HeartFULL
## PET PORTRAITS

Once upon a time, Mellie was living in the Front Range of colorful Colorado when she received a job offer from across the country — near Philadelphia, to be more precise. Although she adored Colorado (and so did her dogs!), she couldn't resist this job offer as a website operations manager and designer with... a PET COMPANY!

So, she packed her 3yo son and 2 dogs in her Prius with all the belongings they could fit, and she moved across the country to take a new job, in a new town, with a new optimism (at that time, the good — and good-paying — jobs in her Colorado town had been seriously lacking).

One of Mellie's favorite things about this new pet company (besides her *wonderful* coworkers) was having REAL LIVE PETS in the office EVERY DAY!  Since the office made use of an open layout, dogs could run around and socialize. Cats would drape across desks. It was HEAVEN for an animal lover like Mellie!

Mellie loved to draw and paint when she was younger, but years ago she'd abandoned her art after (perhaps well-meaning) teachers told her she was neither talented nor special. They were basing their analysis on being able to replicate someone else's work. And at her schools, there was only room for a couple of kids to be deemed "The Artists." So, figuring they knew best, she listened, and didn't pick up a pencil or paintbrush for ages. Luckily, after college, Mellie discovered and taught herself graphic design, which became a creative outlet in the interim between then... and now. (Although there was a near birth of HeartFULL Pet Portraits around 2007 when Mellie created a portrait of her sister's Rottie in this bold and funky style as a birthday gift.  There wasn't any strategy around this line-art-meets-watercolor creation — it simply happened! Mellie's sister Tara displays the very first HeartFULL Pet Portrait to this day.)

After an astrology reading with and encouragement from a talented woman named Wendy Cicchetti in 2013, Mellie realized that the "missing piece" in her life was indeed her creative expression, and decided to challenge herself to create again. Every day, she committed to just 30 minutes, to relieve the pressure of creating something "perfect."

So, she allowed herself to begin creating. For 30 minutes each morning, Mellie would draw and paint, and the obvious choice for a subject was... pets! She began drawing the adorable #junecarterdog as her first experiment.   Using only a Sharpie and some watercolor to keep things simple, Mellie created.. and then shared.

A Boston Terrier named Franklin and a cat named Daisy were next.  Mellie began gifting her coworkers with these quick pet portrait pieces, and soon she began to get requests. A couple years later, after moving back to Colorado, Mellie realized she was actually connecting with the energy of each animal, just as in proper animal communication. She then realized that these were no ordinary portraits; they were magical and actually ENCHANTED!

Since that time, these magical HeartFULL Pet Portraits have expanded into custom necklace charms, oracle decks, tee shirt designs, and now, a COLORING BOOK!  Of course, Mellie's style has continued to evolve over the last 2.5 years, and this coloring book contains a selection of her earliest dog portraits alongside her most recent (this month)! She really hopes you enjoy the magic and wisdom and soulful connection that each of these dogs have to share with you!

# BAILEY

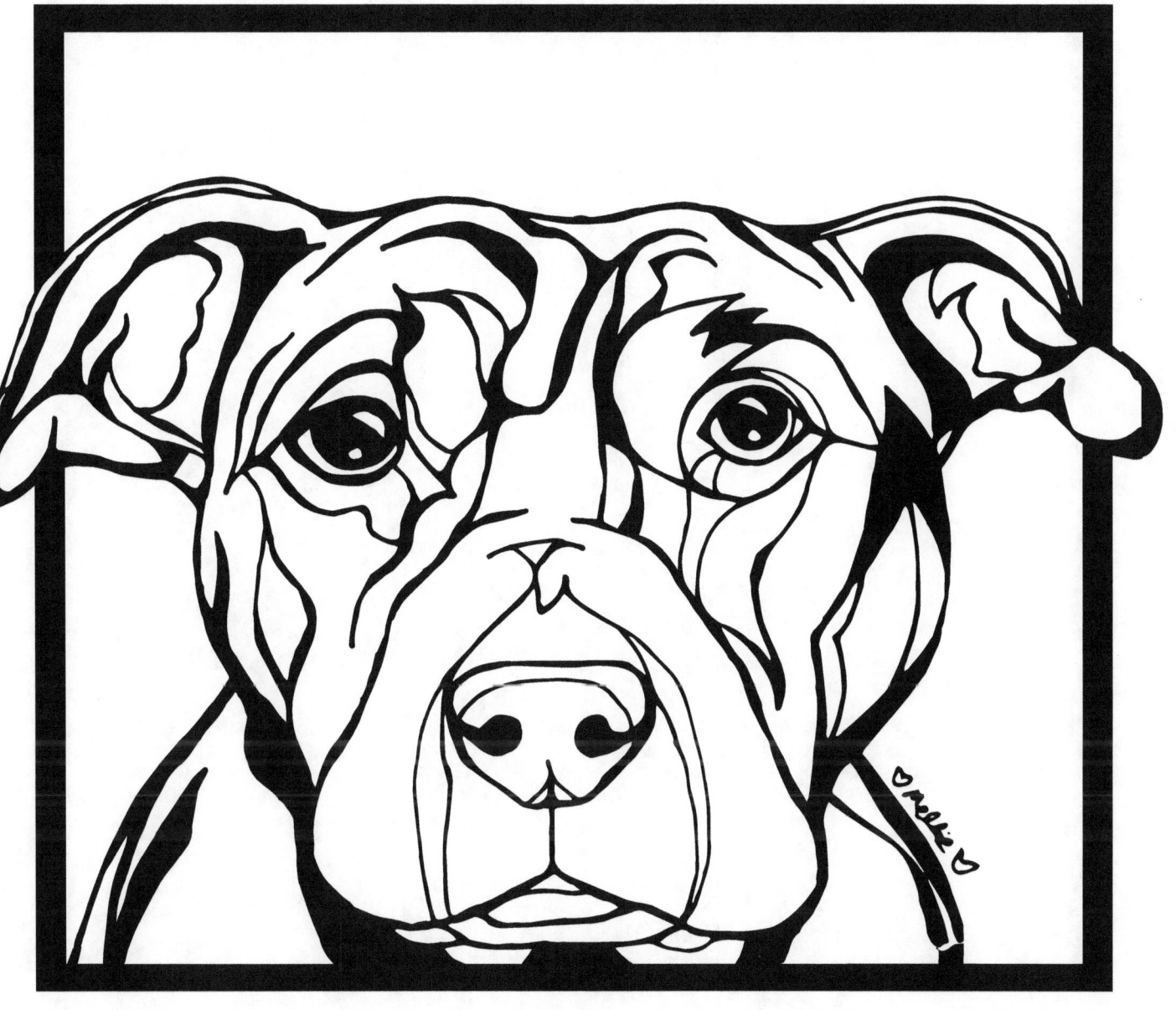

# BAILEY

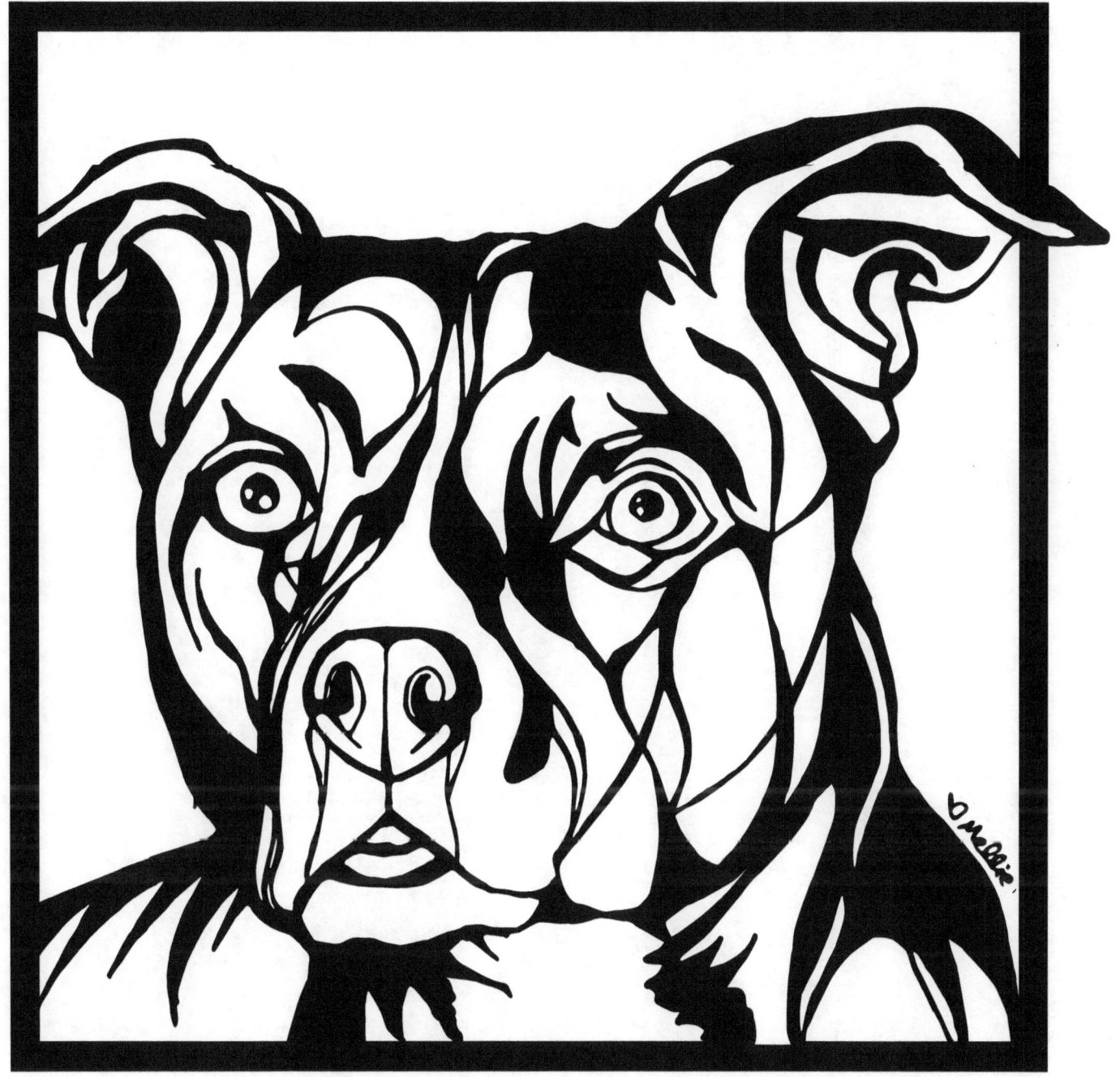

# BOGEY

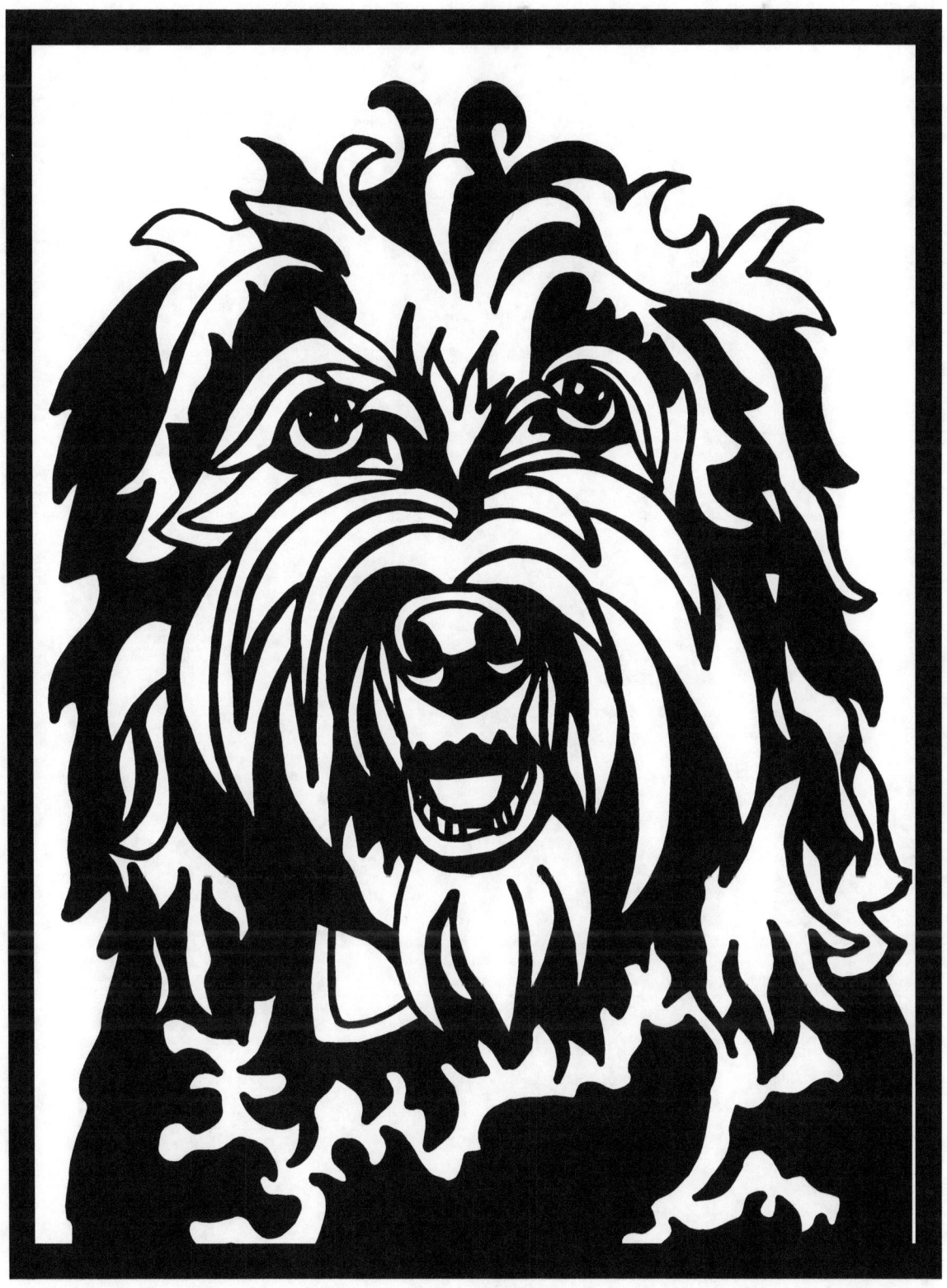

# BRUTIS

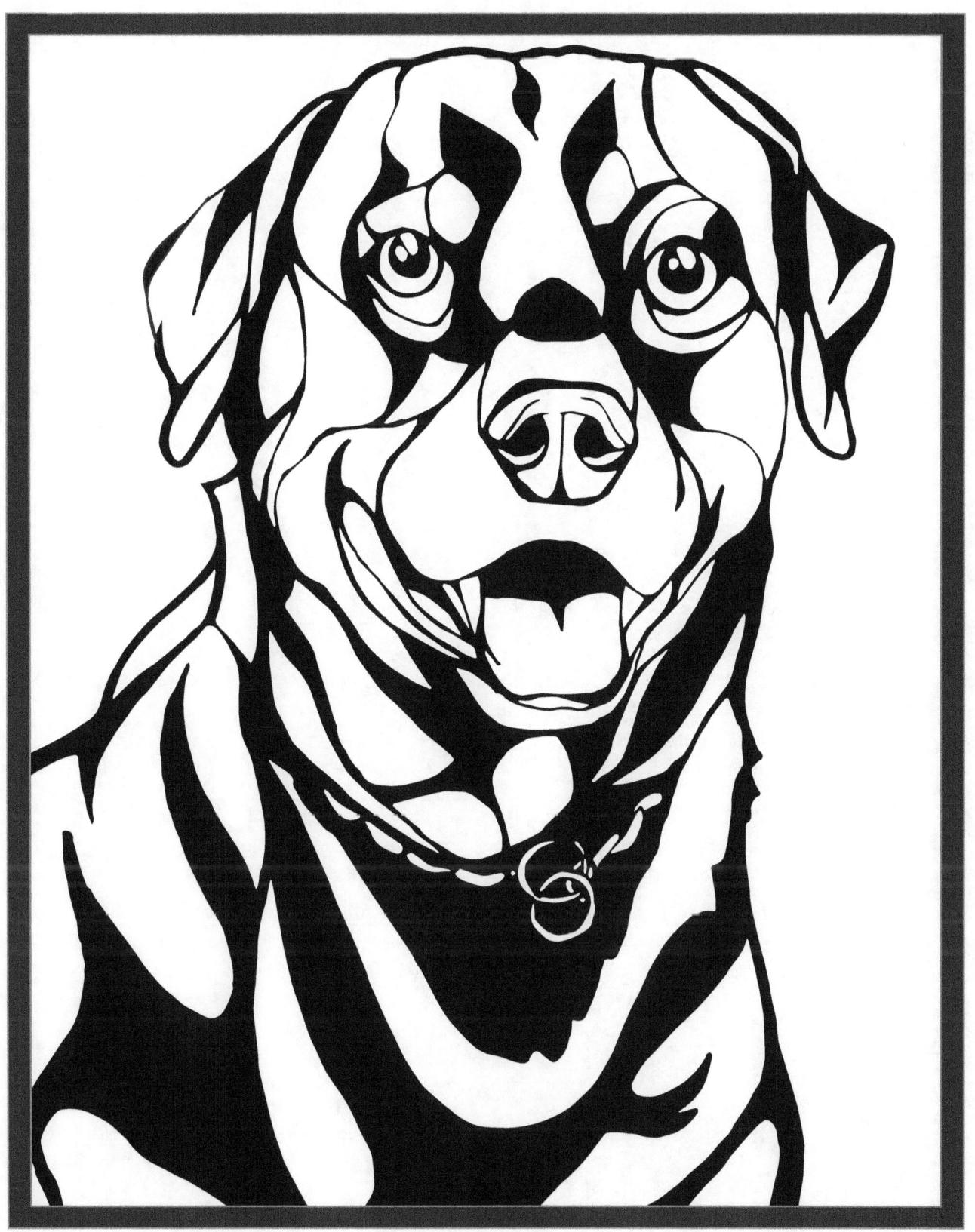

# CHUPACABRA

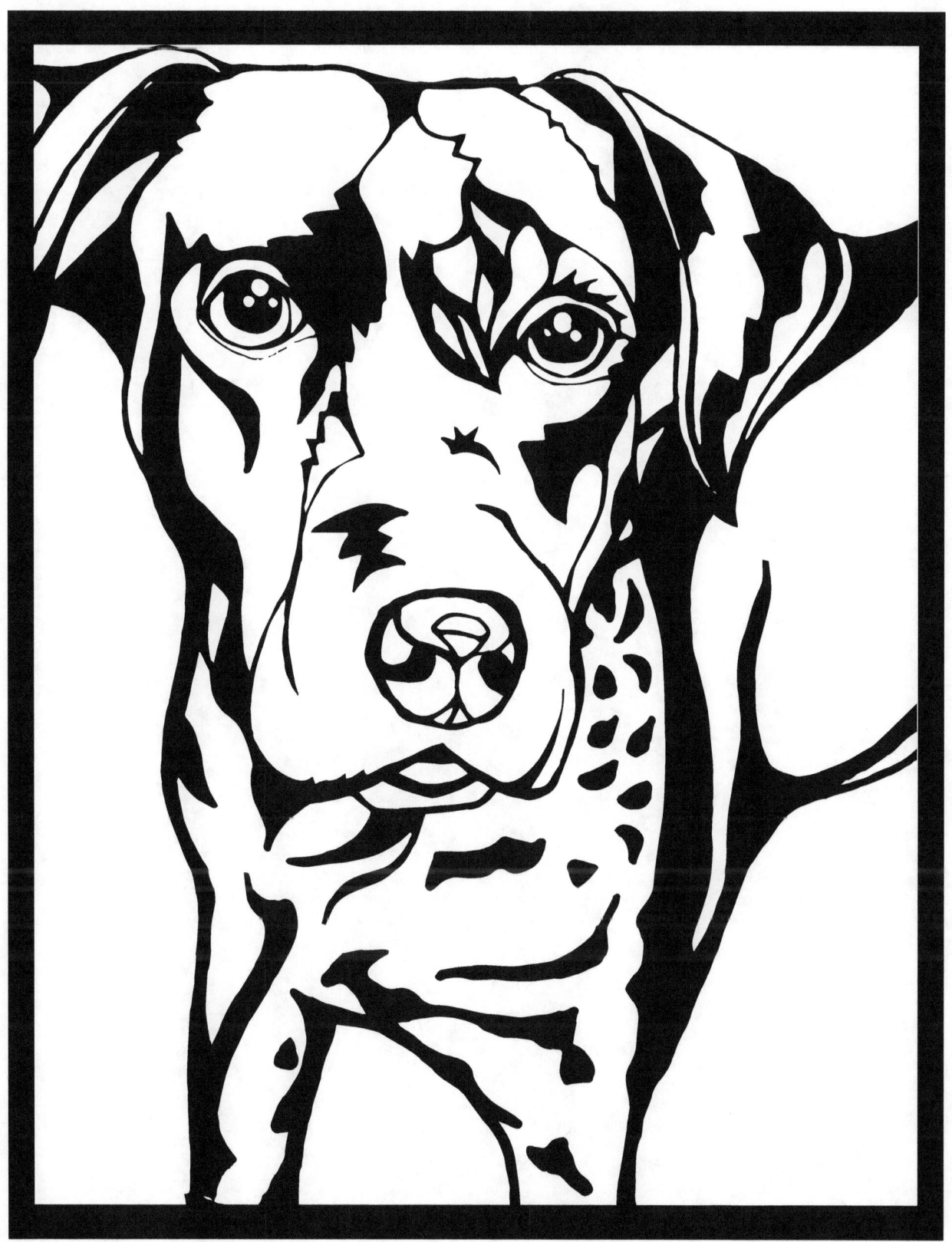

# COSMO

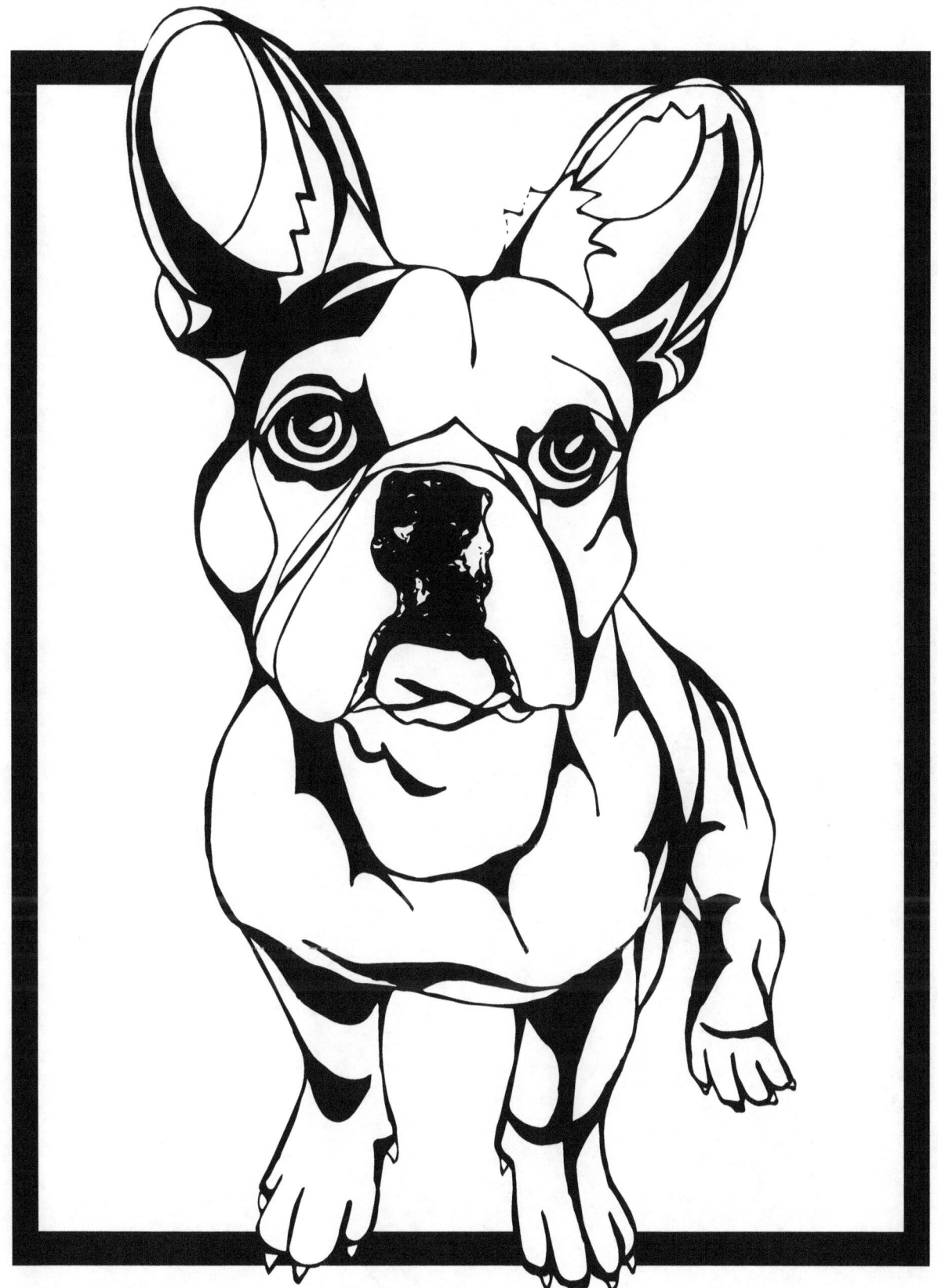

# ELI

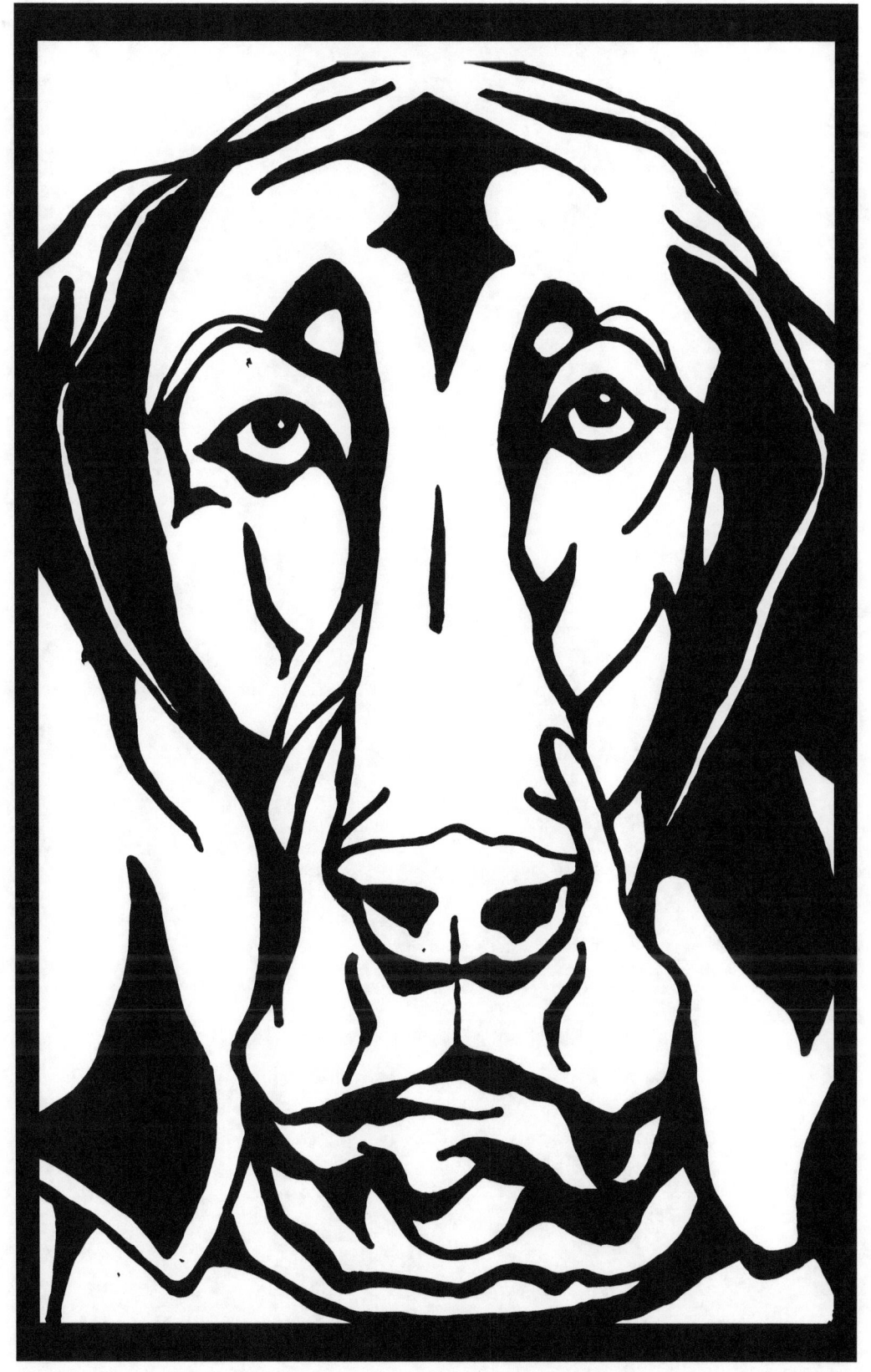

# ELPHIE

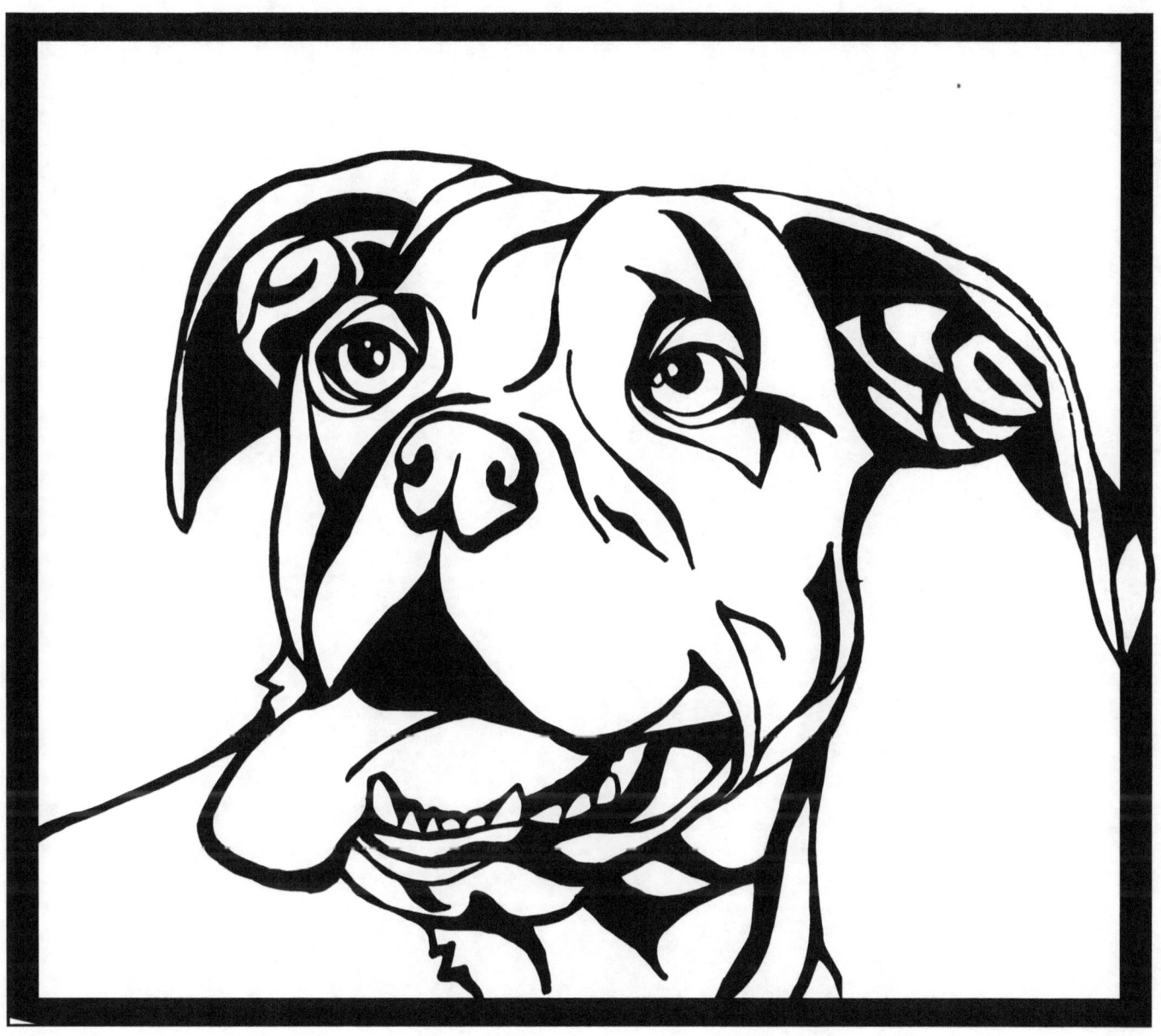

# EMILY, CHESTER MOLLY and OLIVE

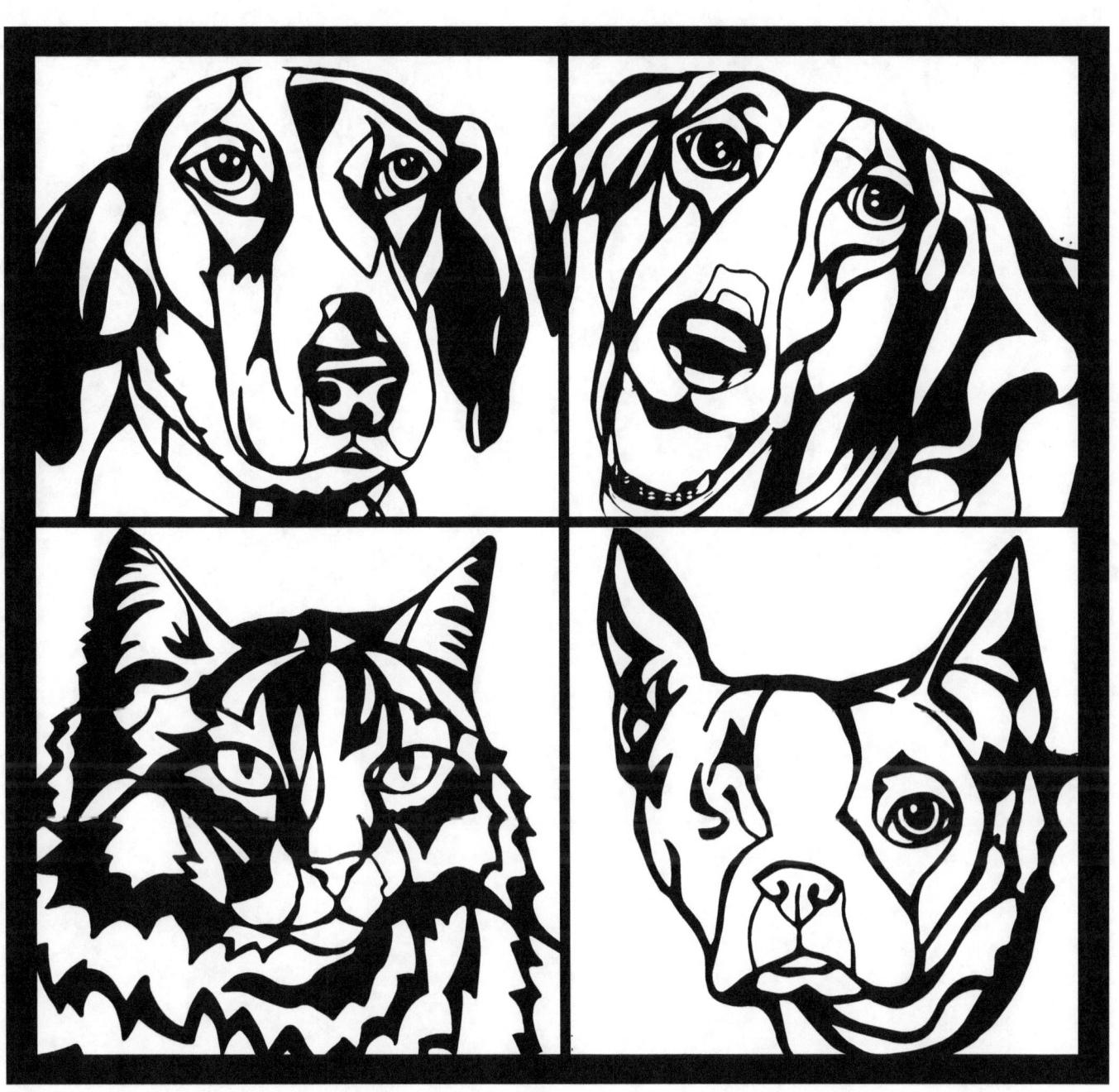

# GEORGE

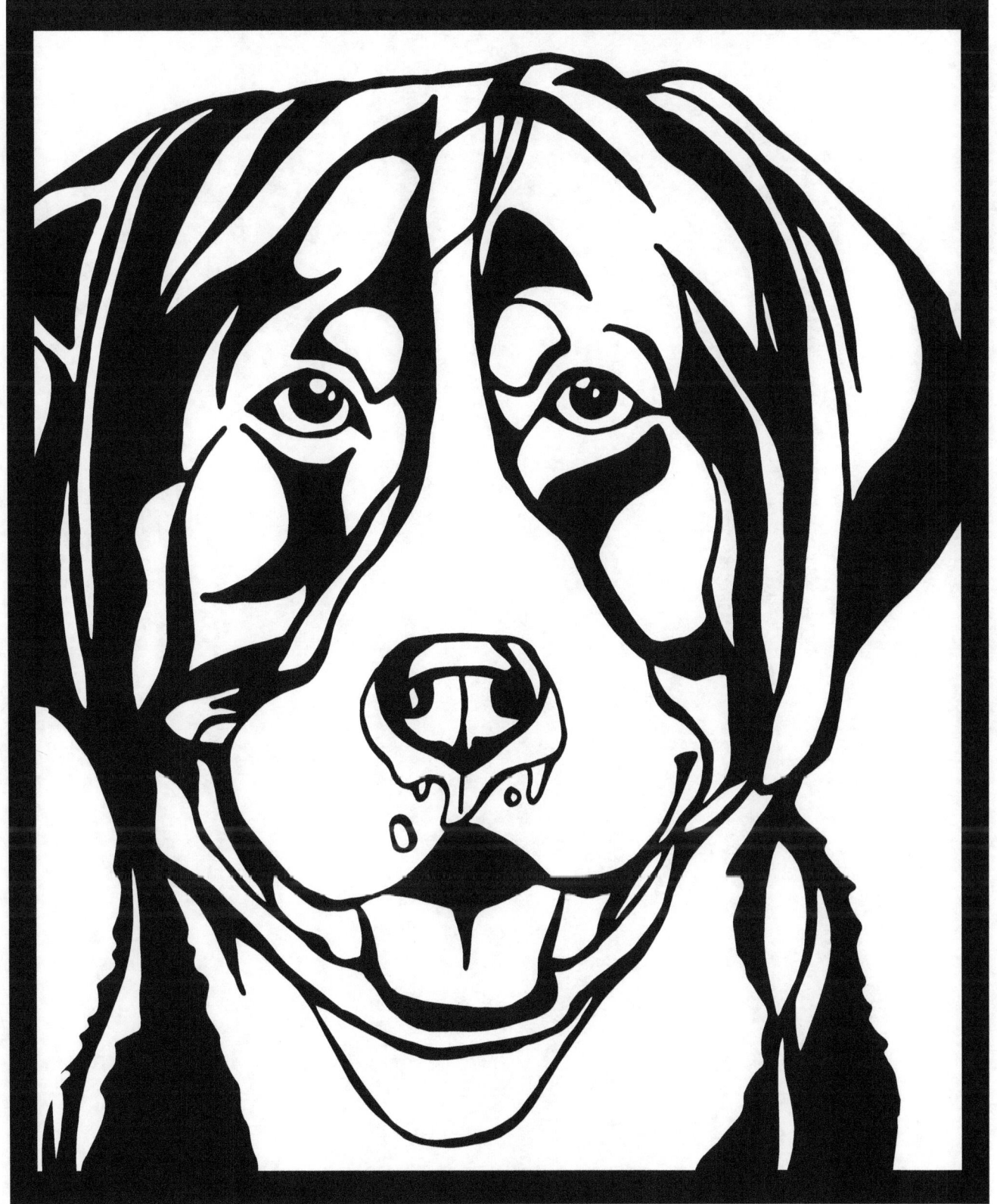

# GUS

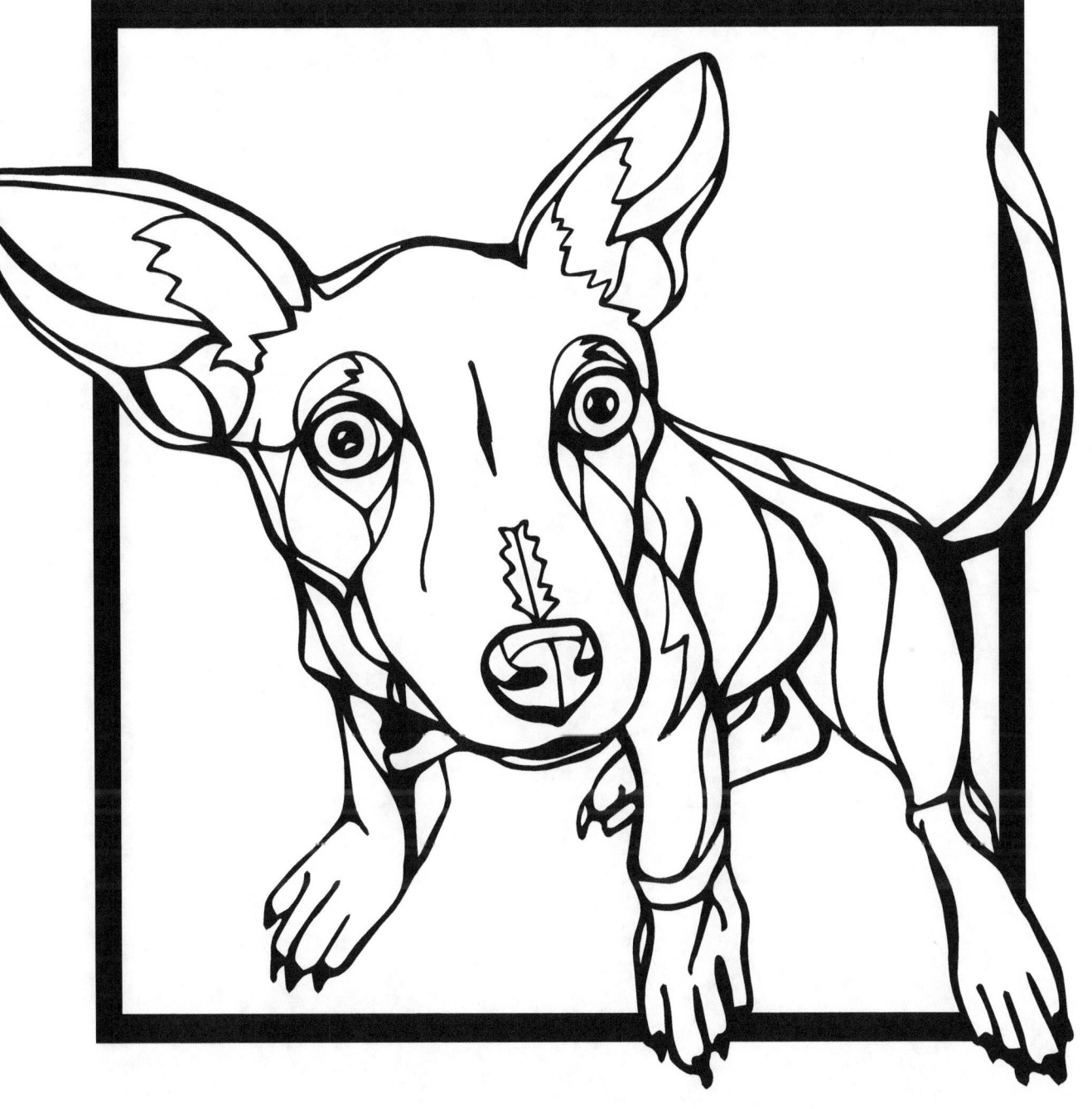

# JAKE

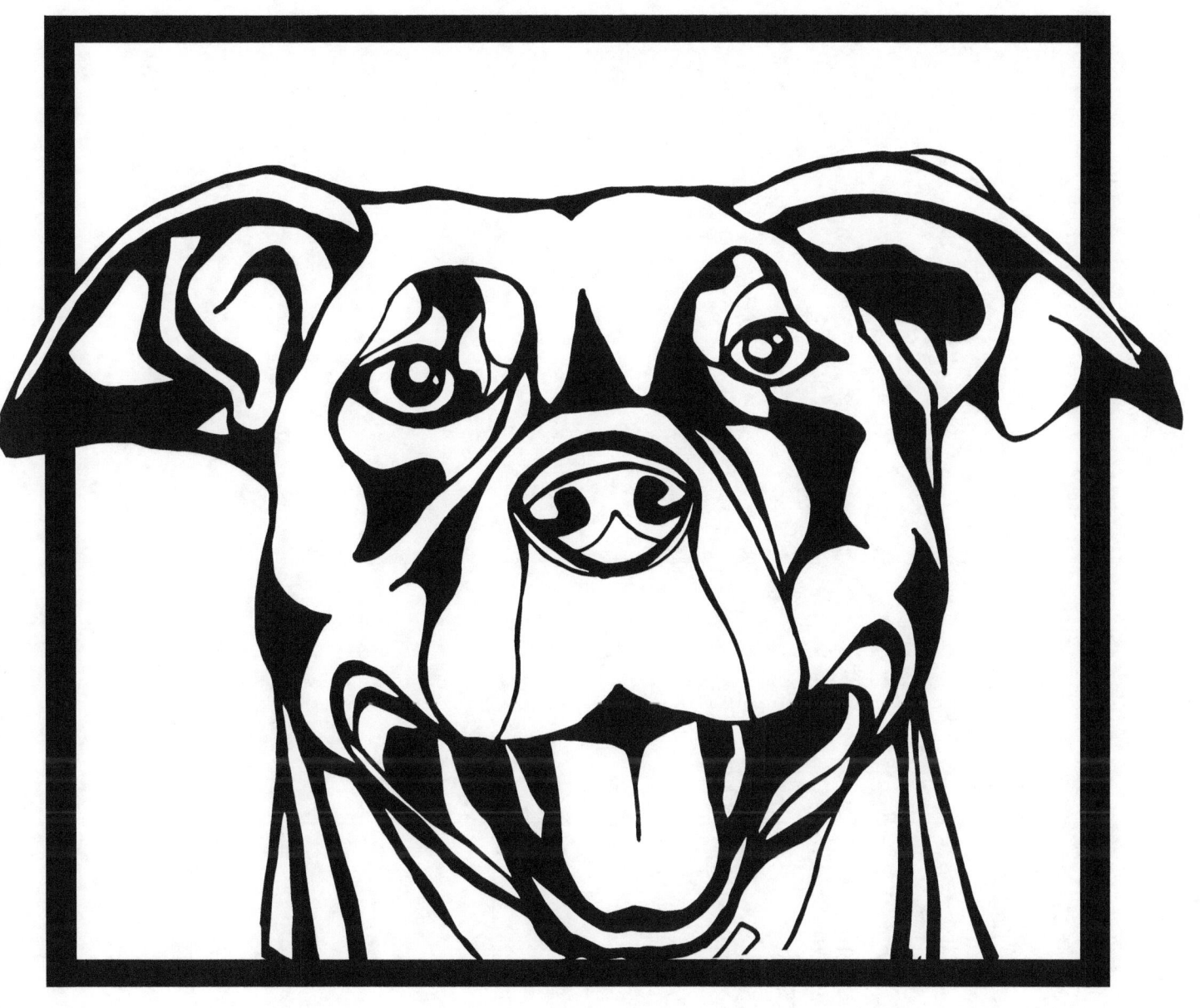

# "THE JAKE"

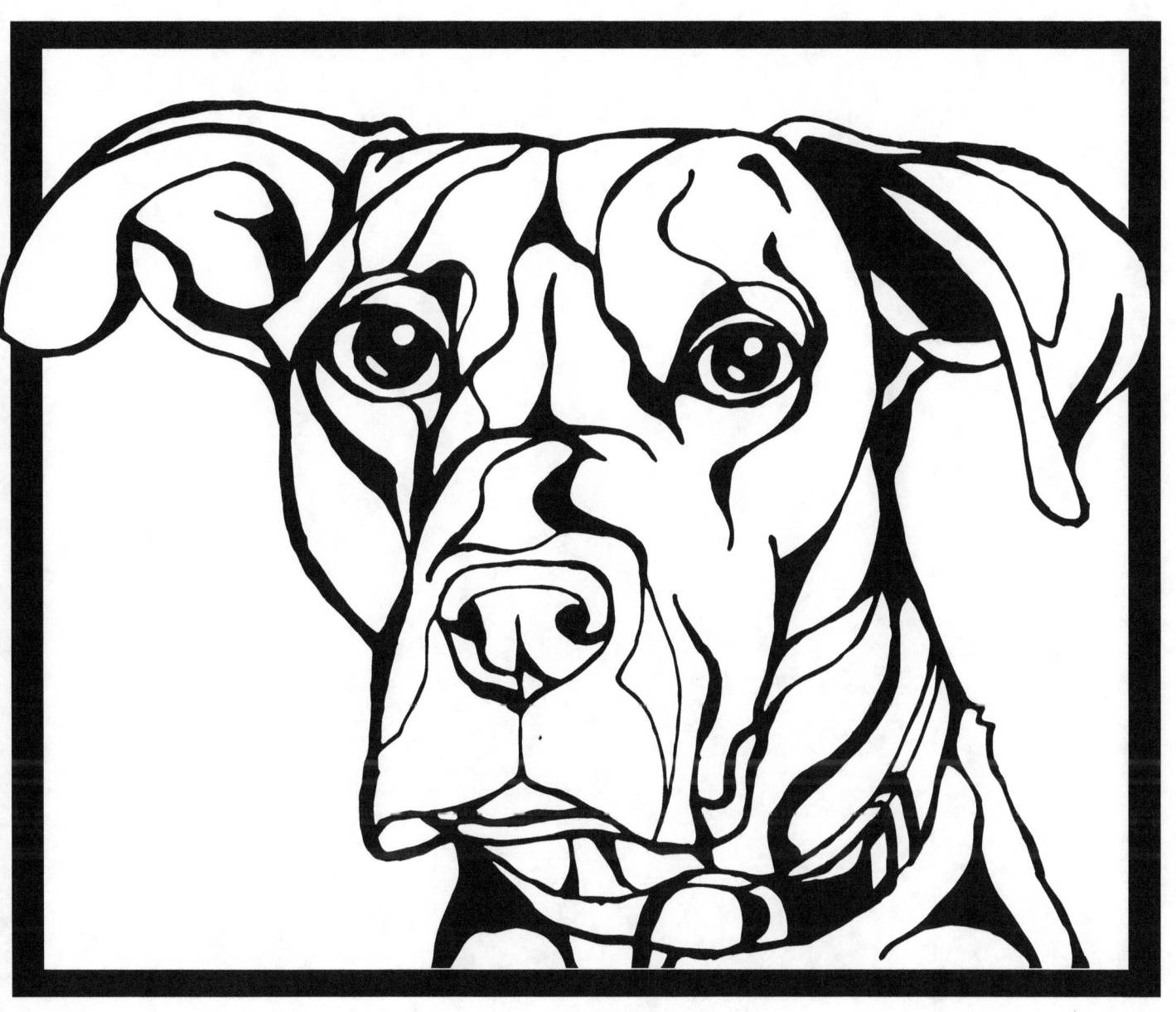

# KIA

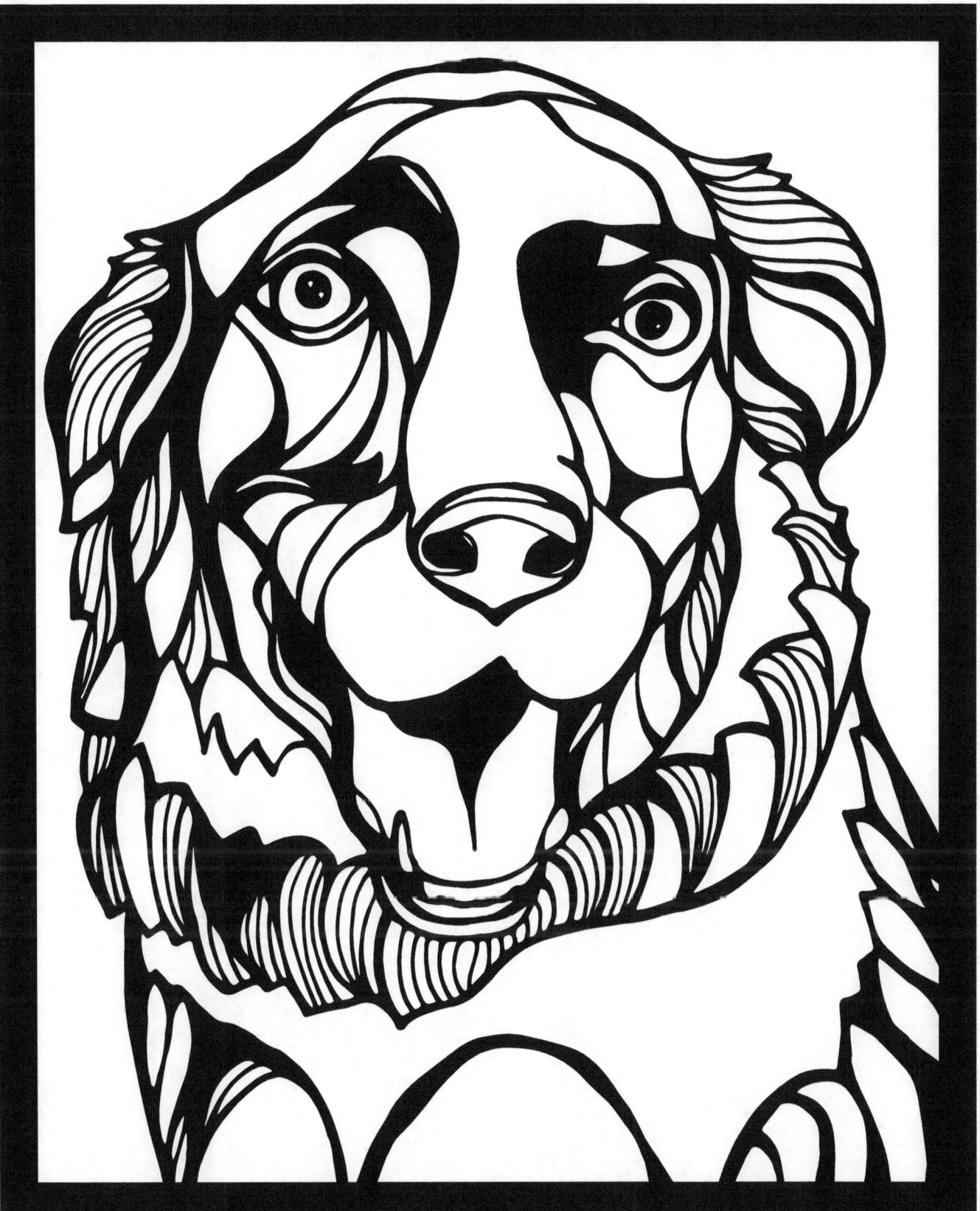

# KULO

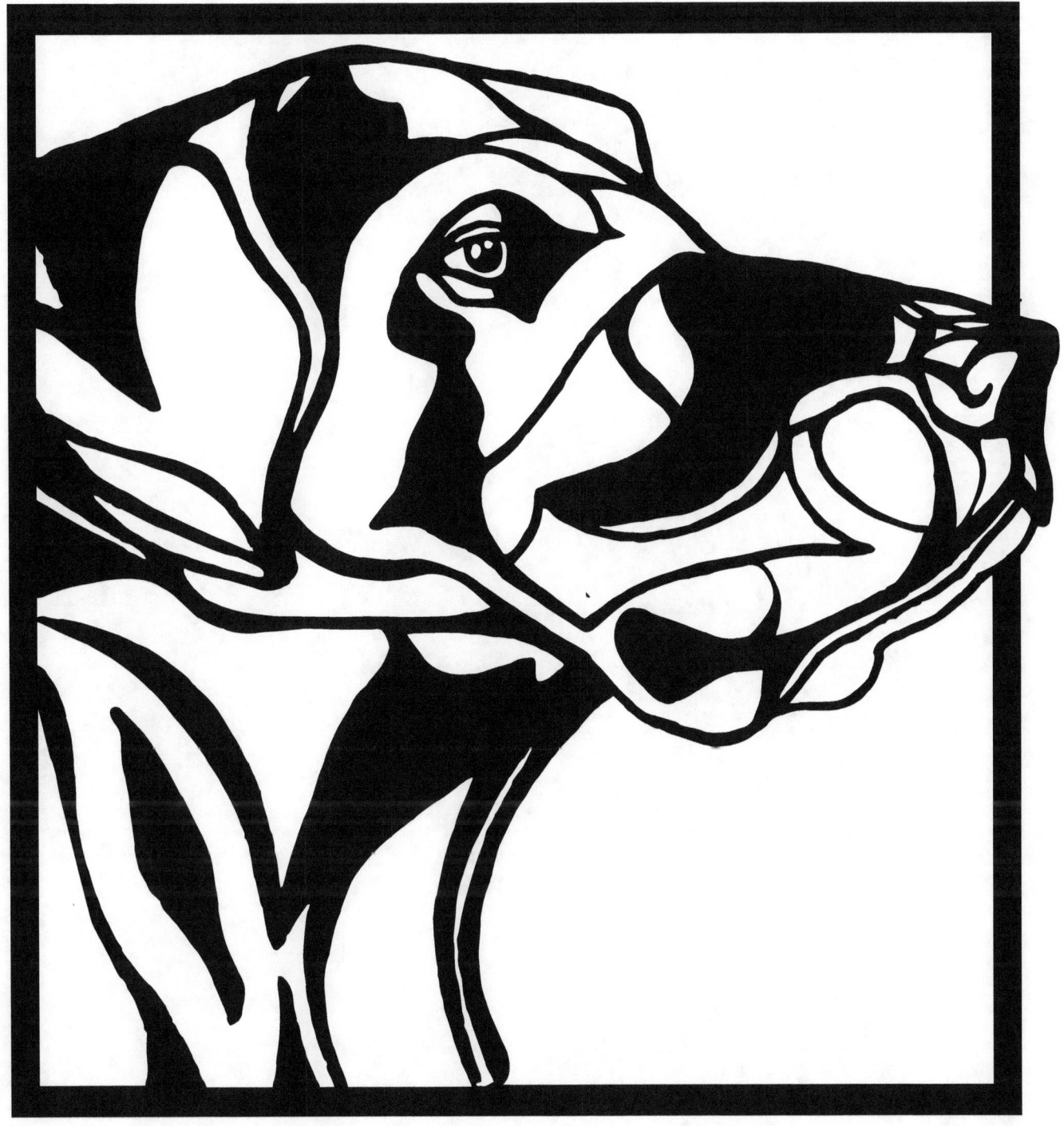

# LUCA

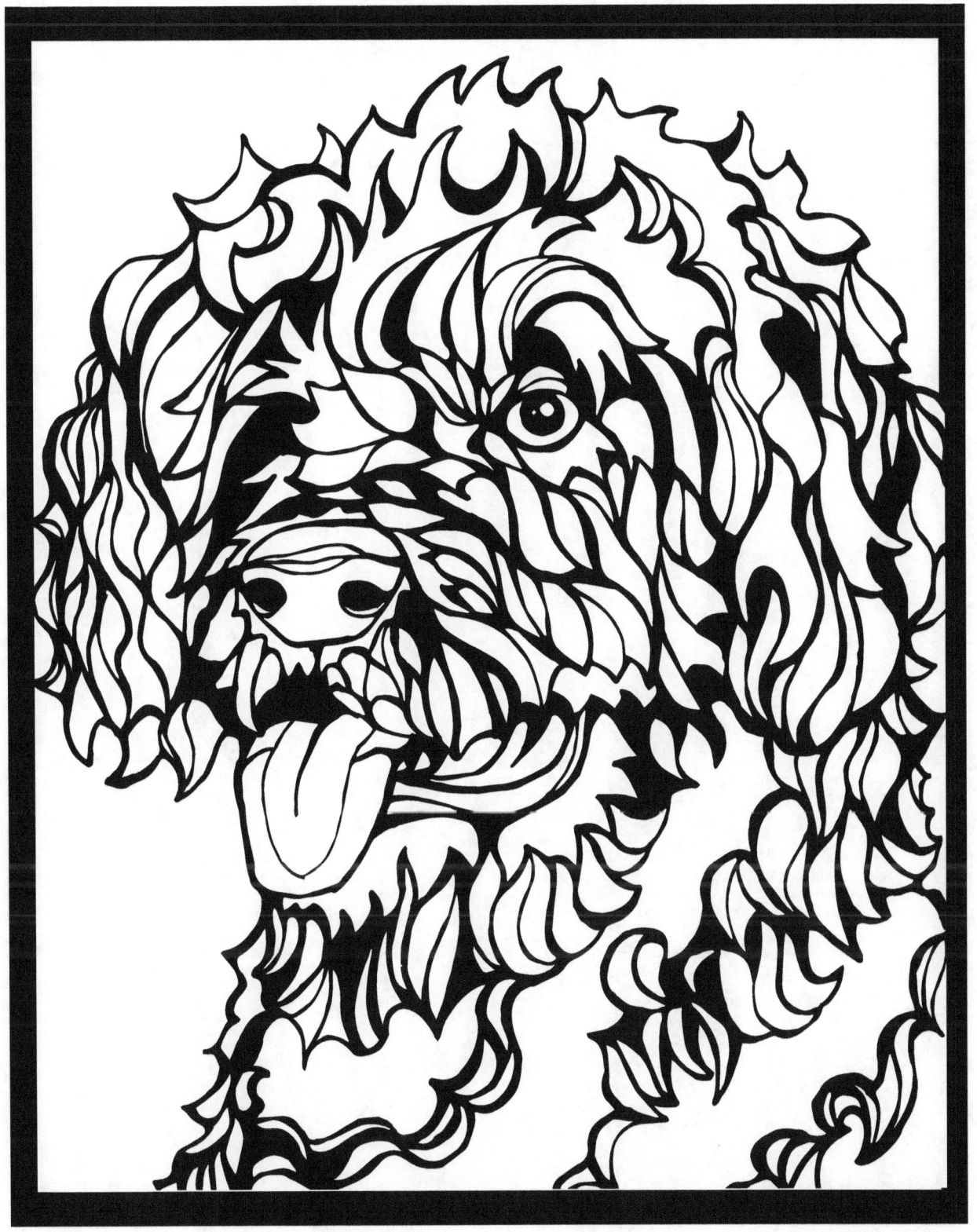

# LUDO

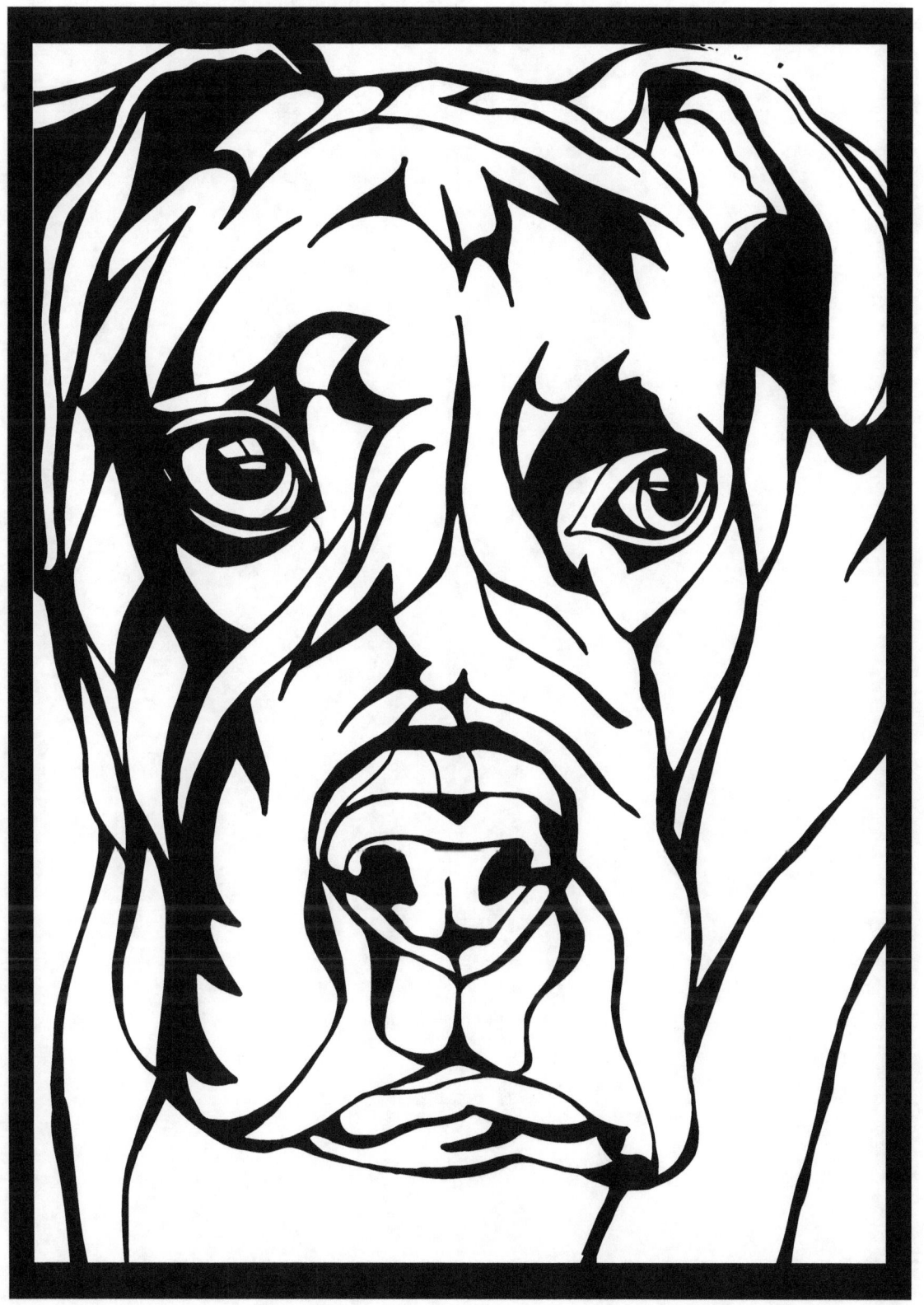

# LULU

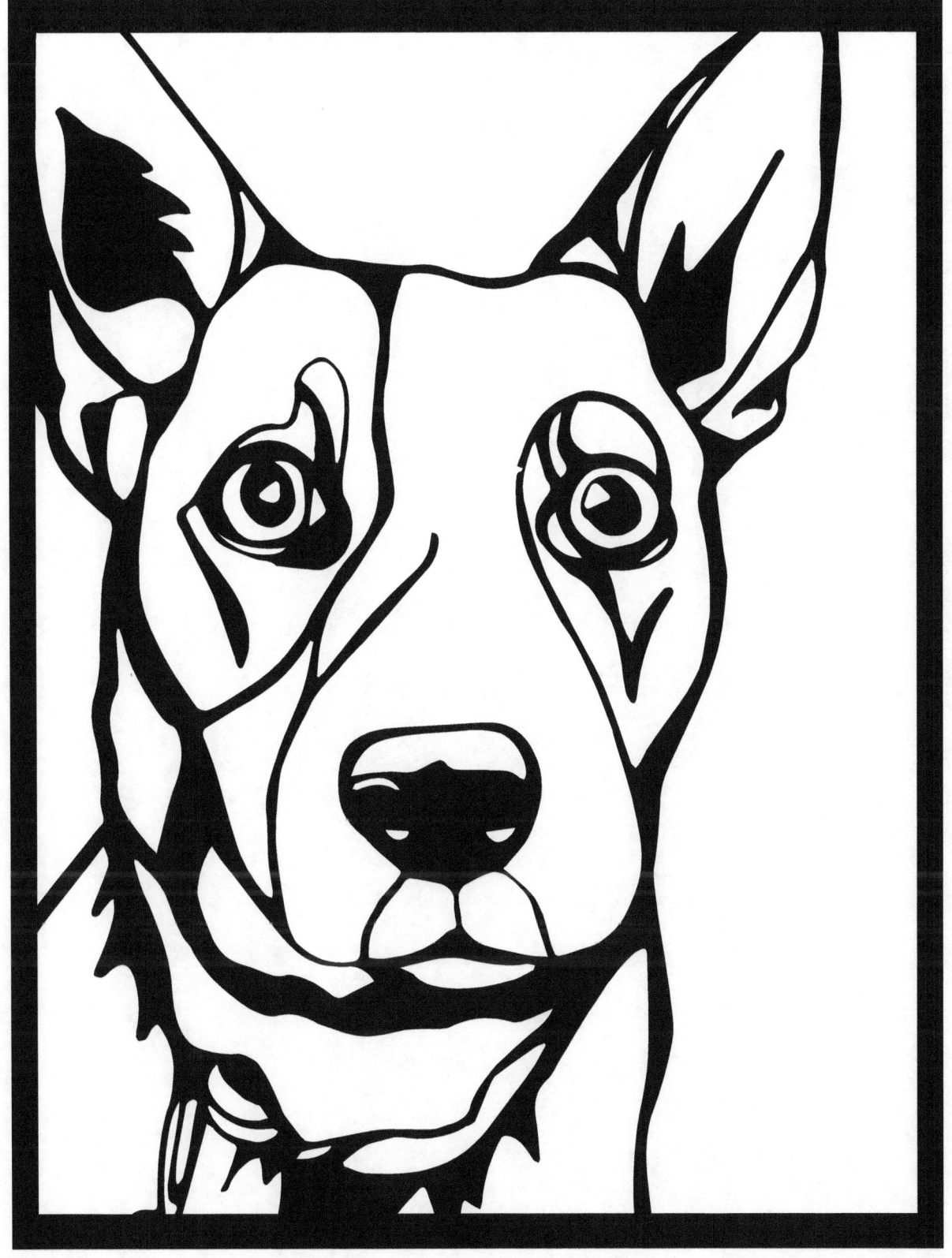

# MADDIE

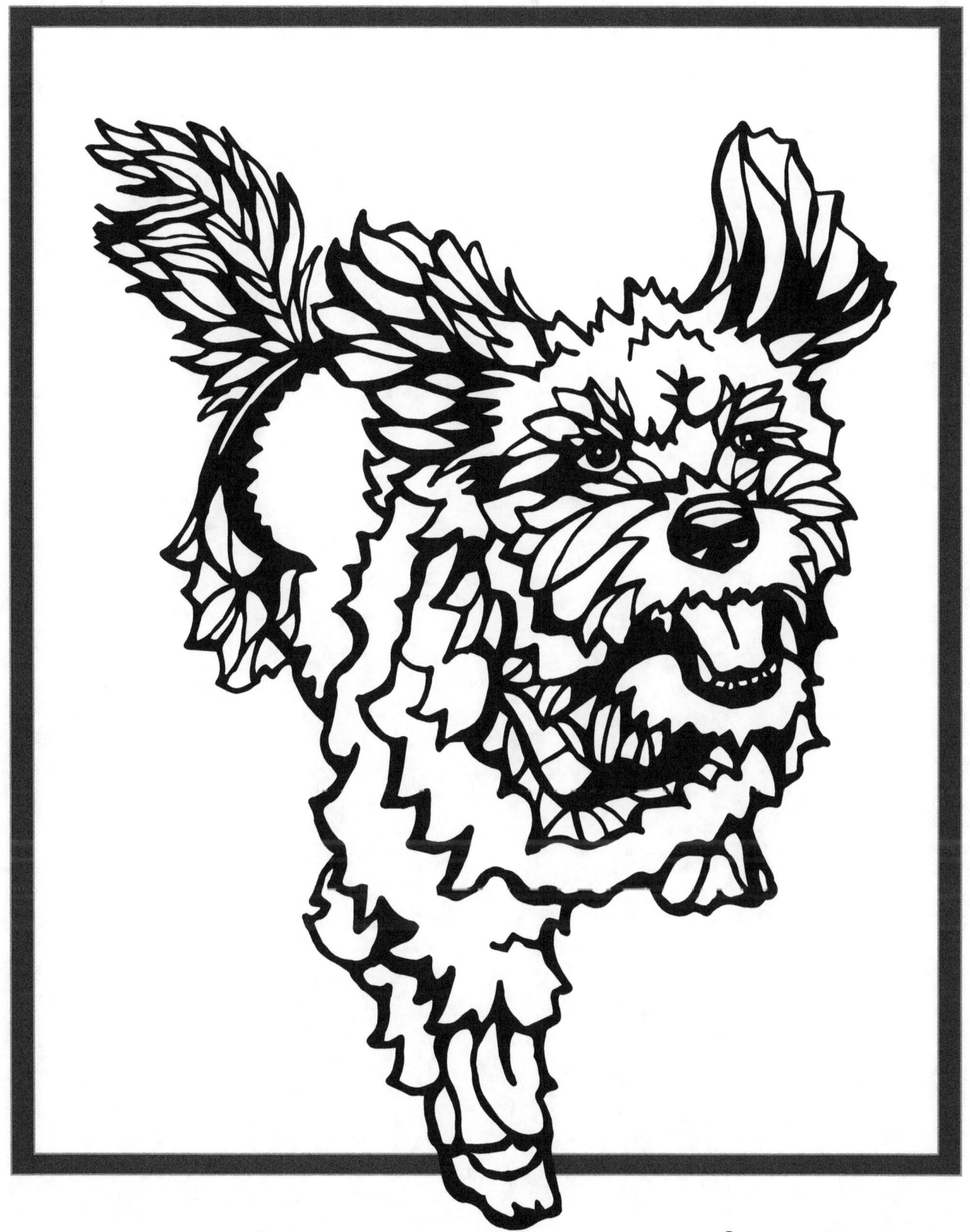

# MAIA

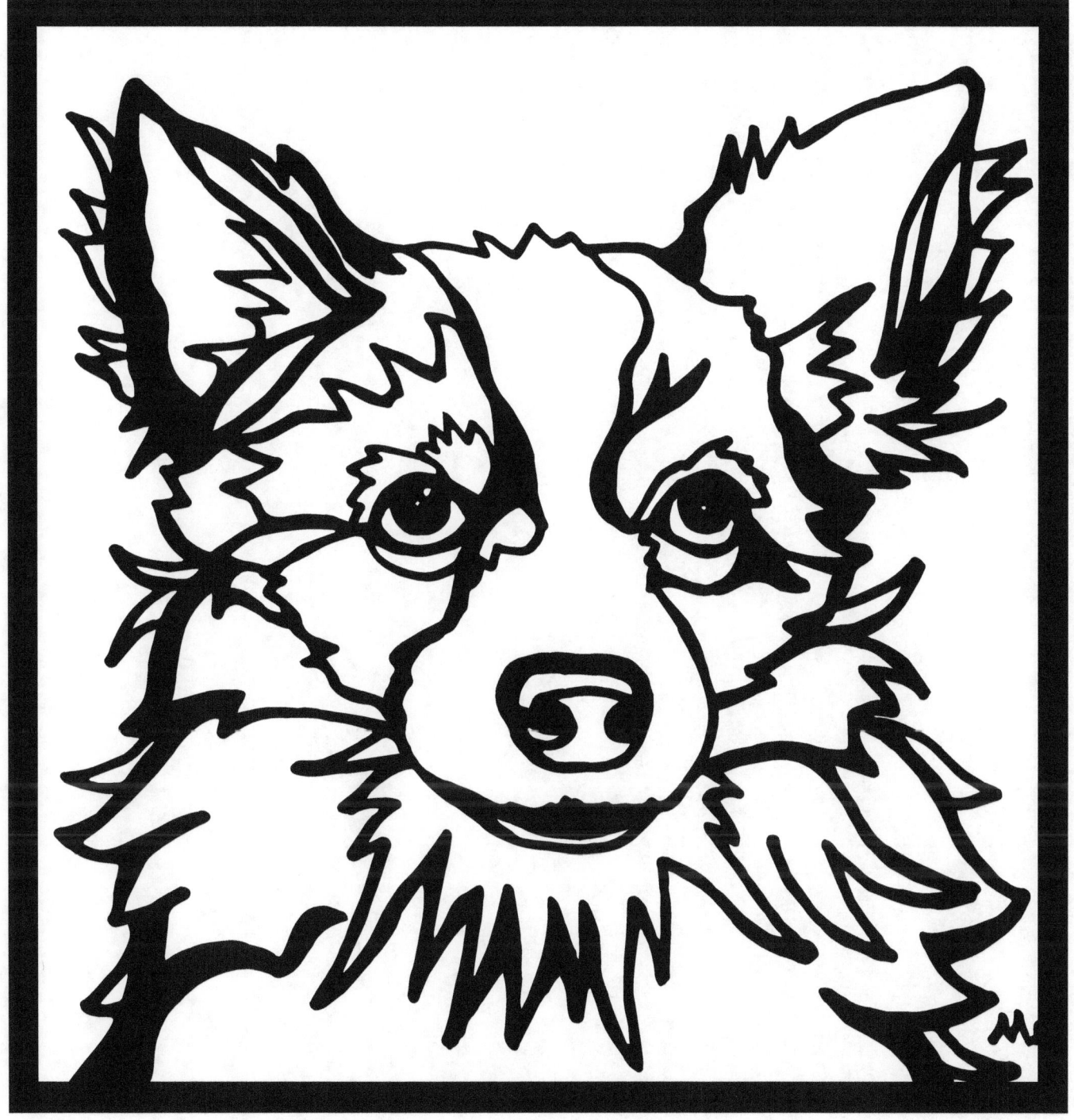

# MATTIE

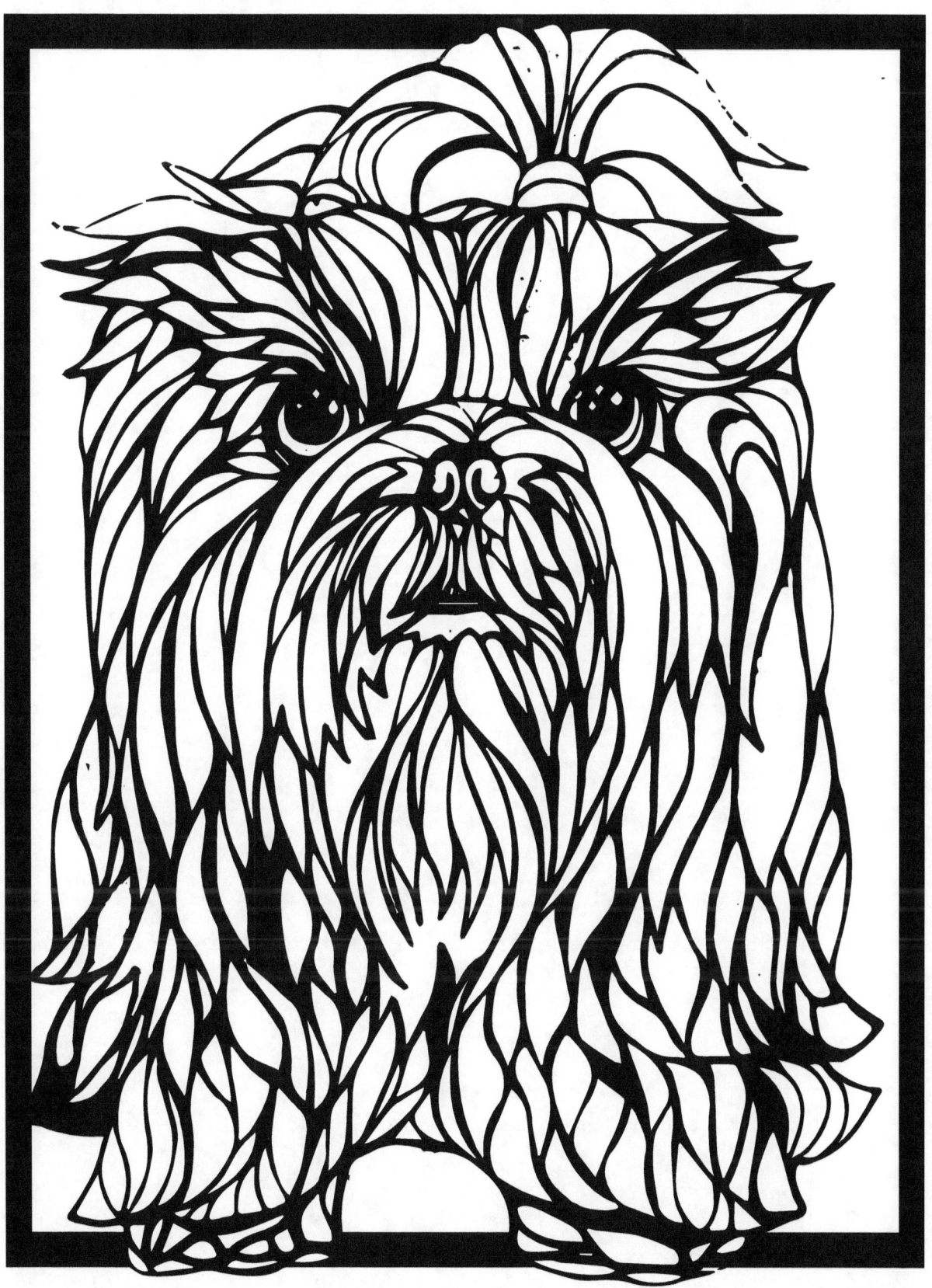

# NEO

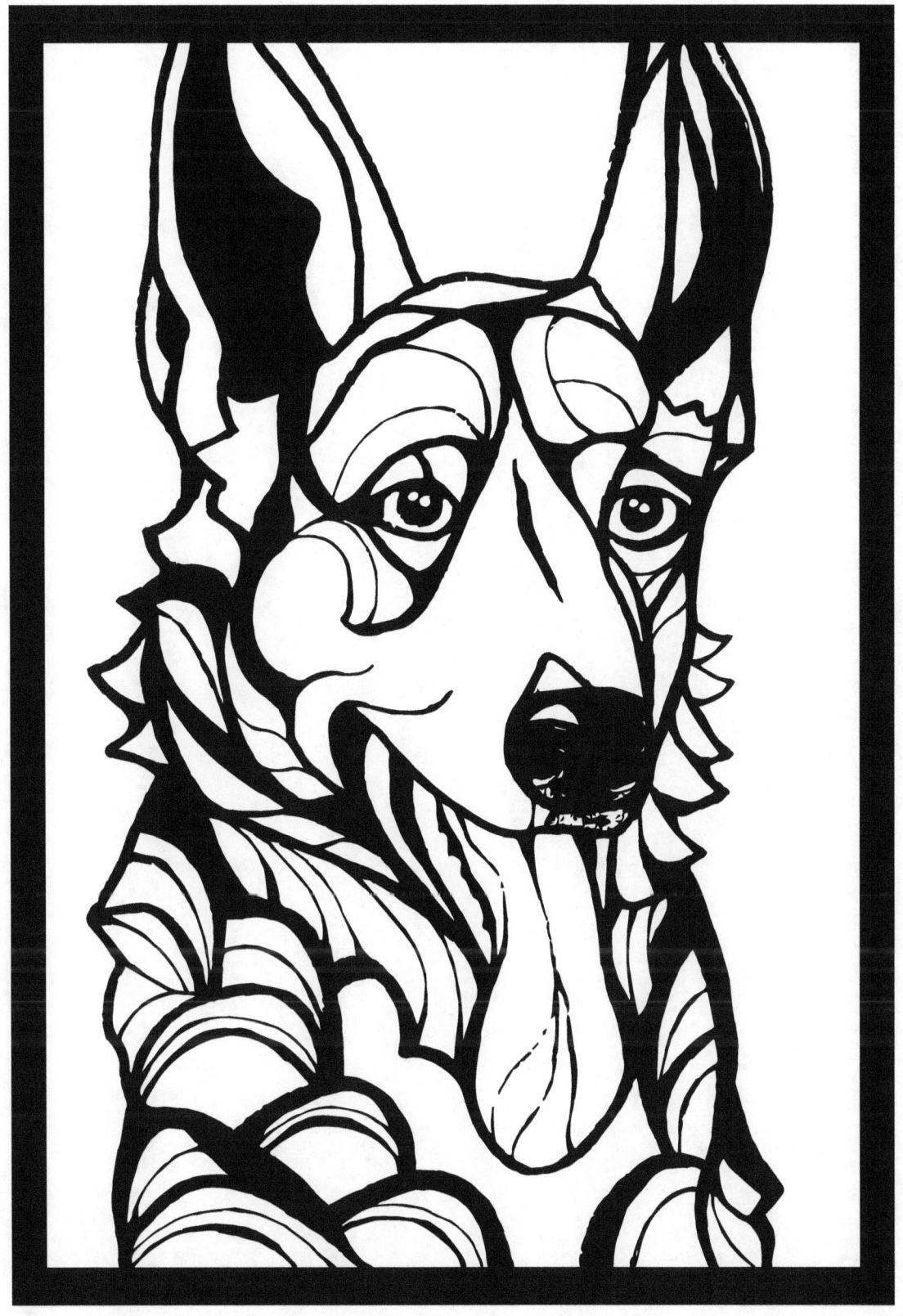

# NYSHA

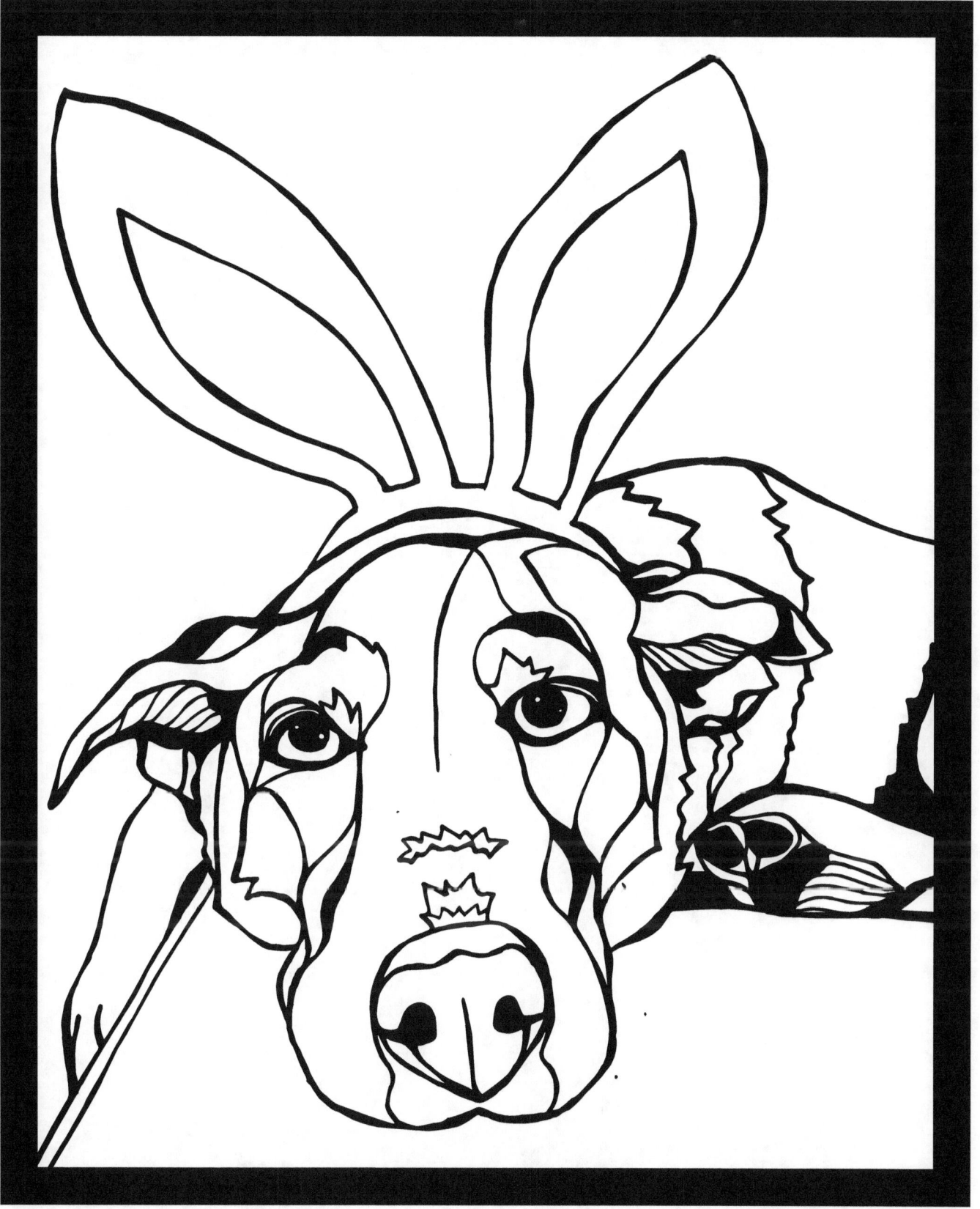

# OPIE

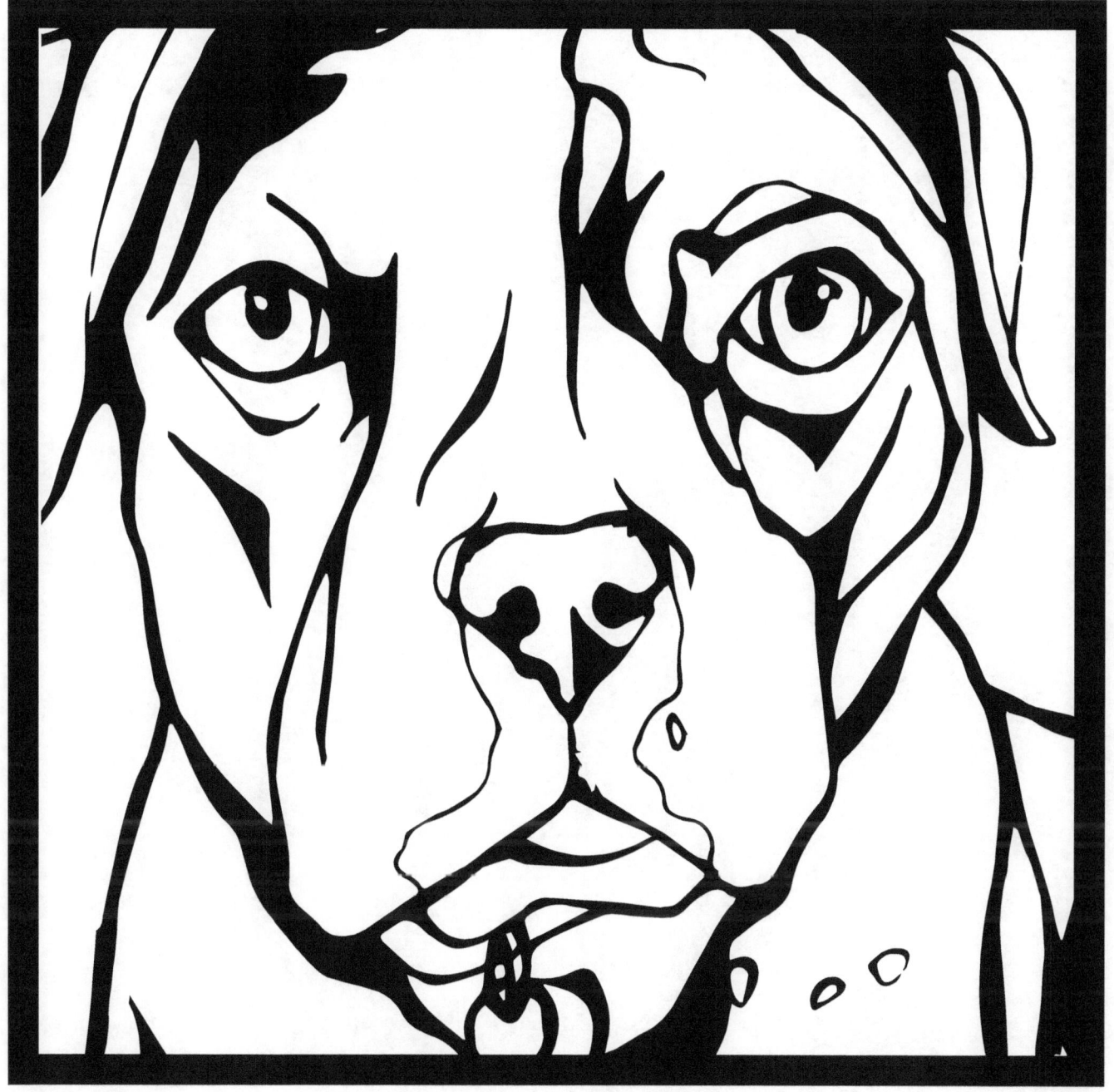

# OREO

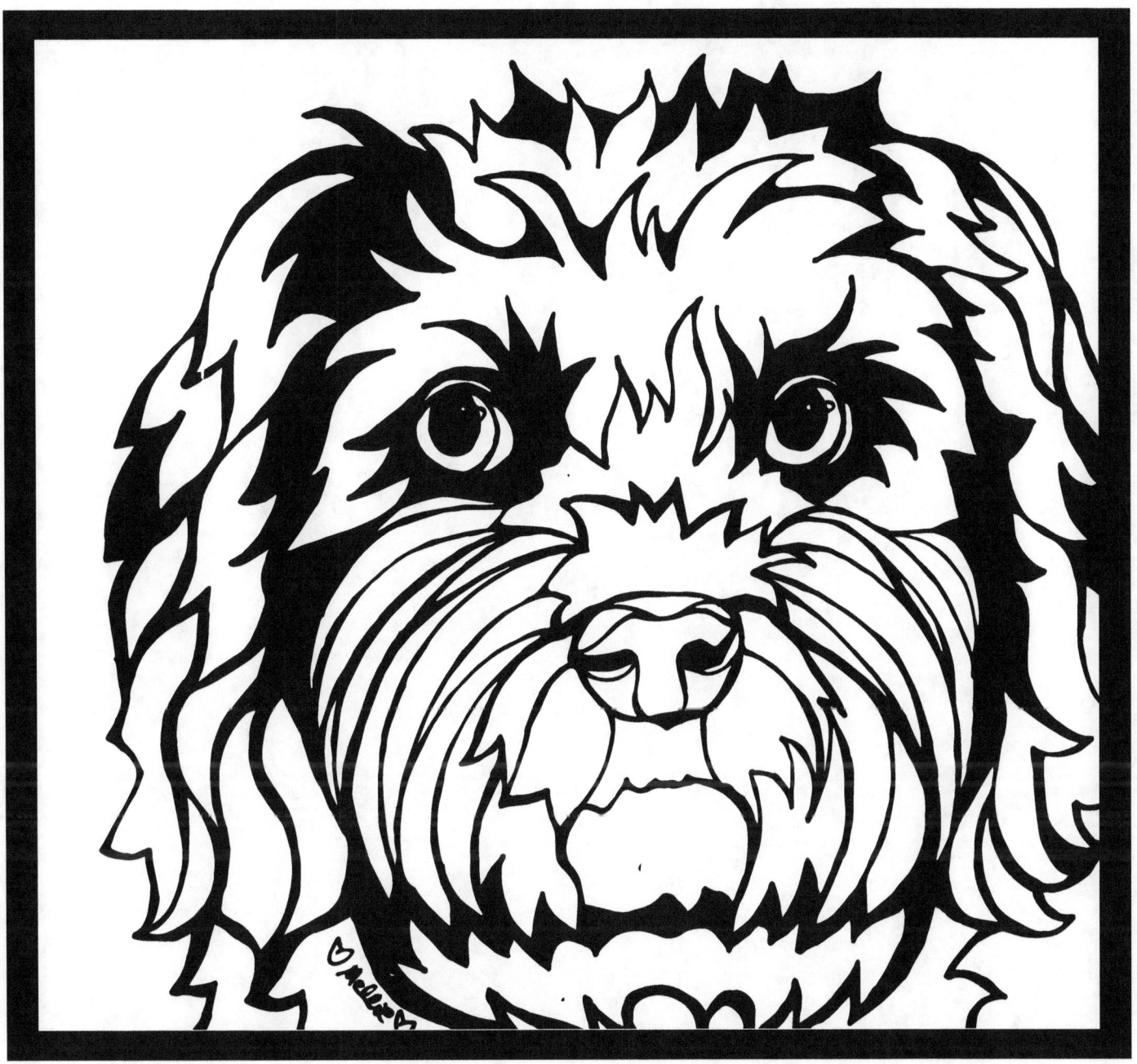

# PENNY

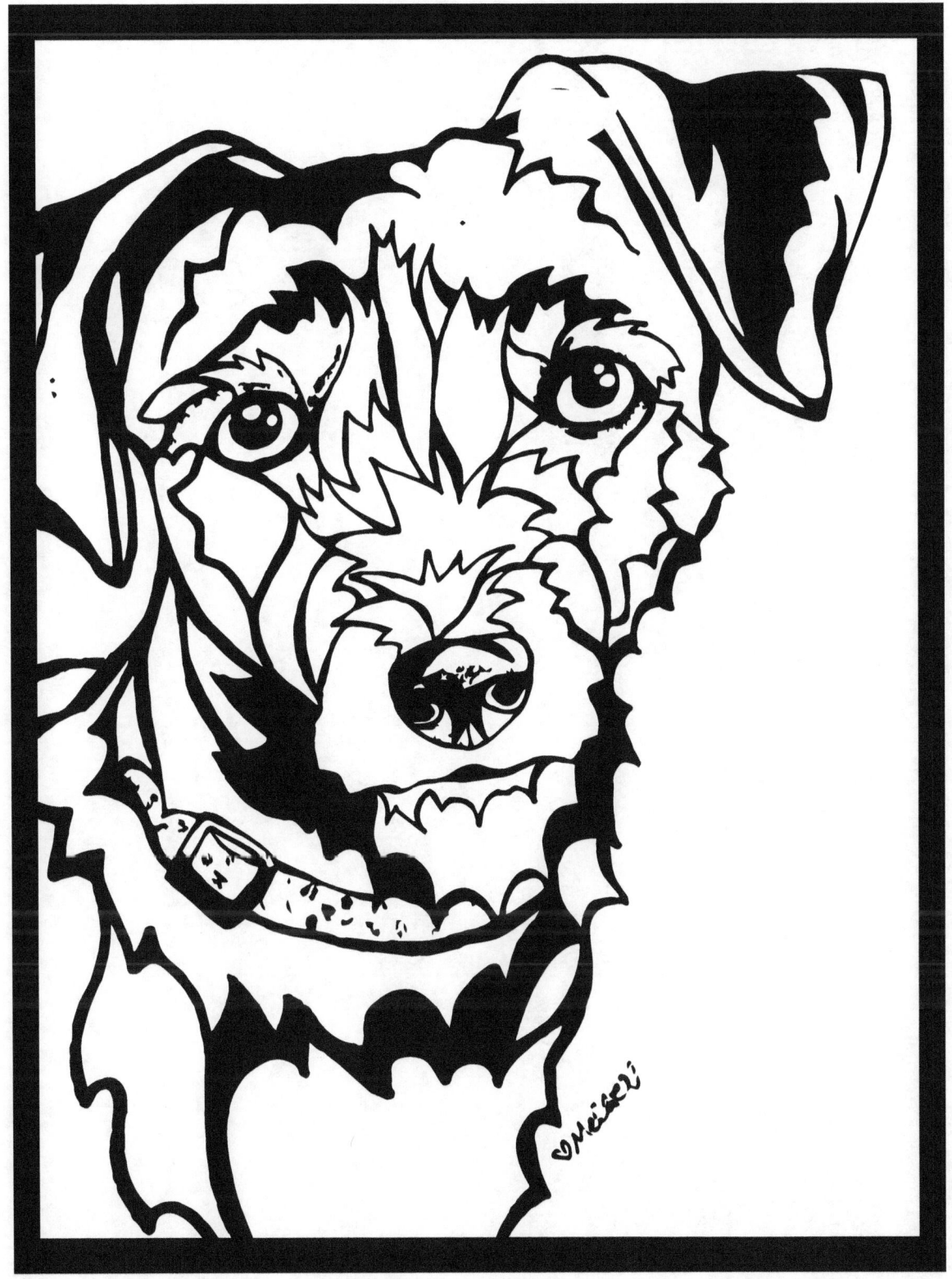

# PIPER

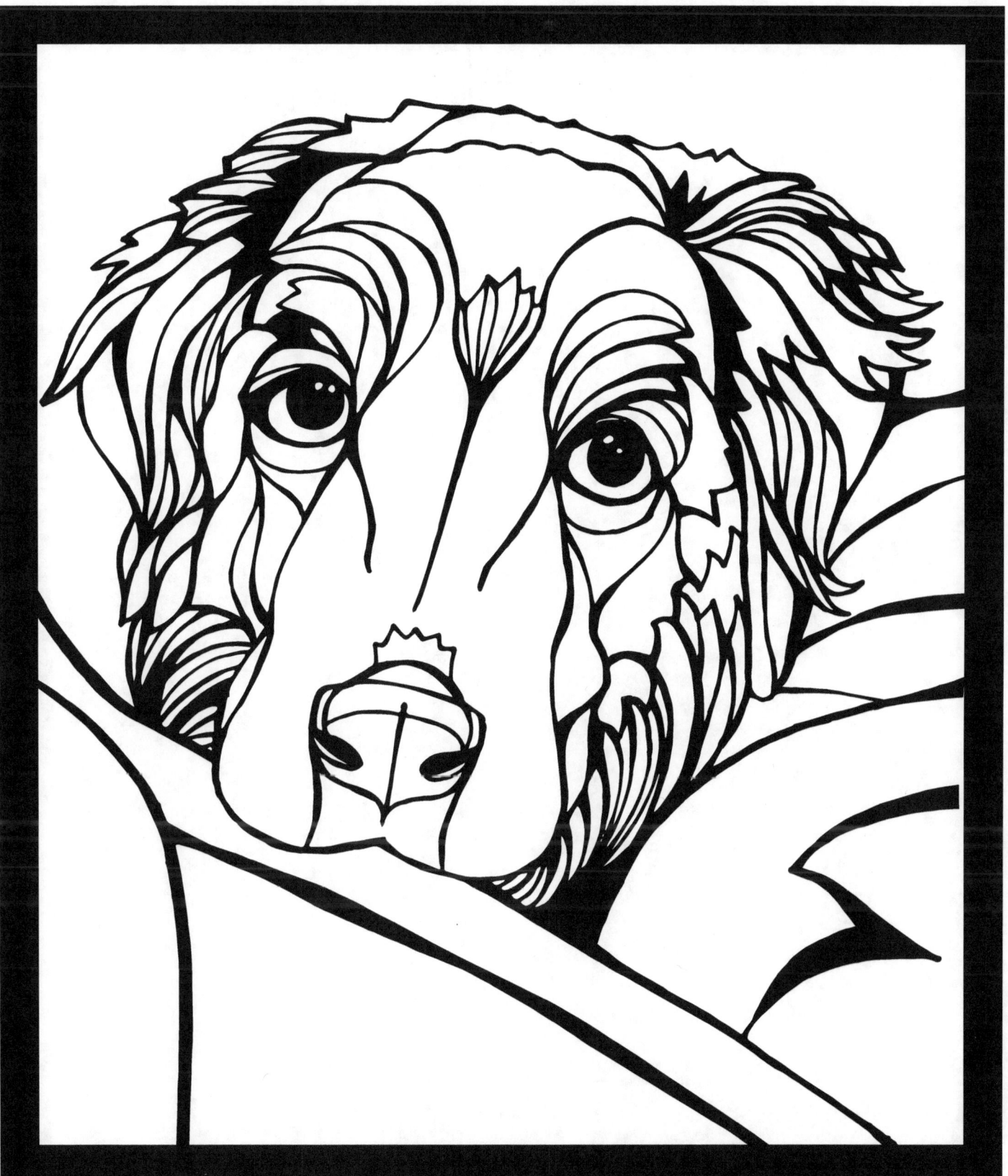

# RUBY

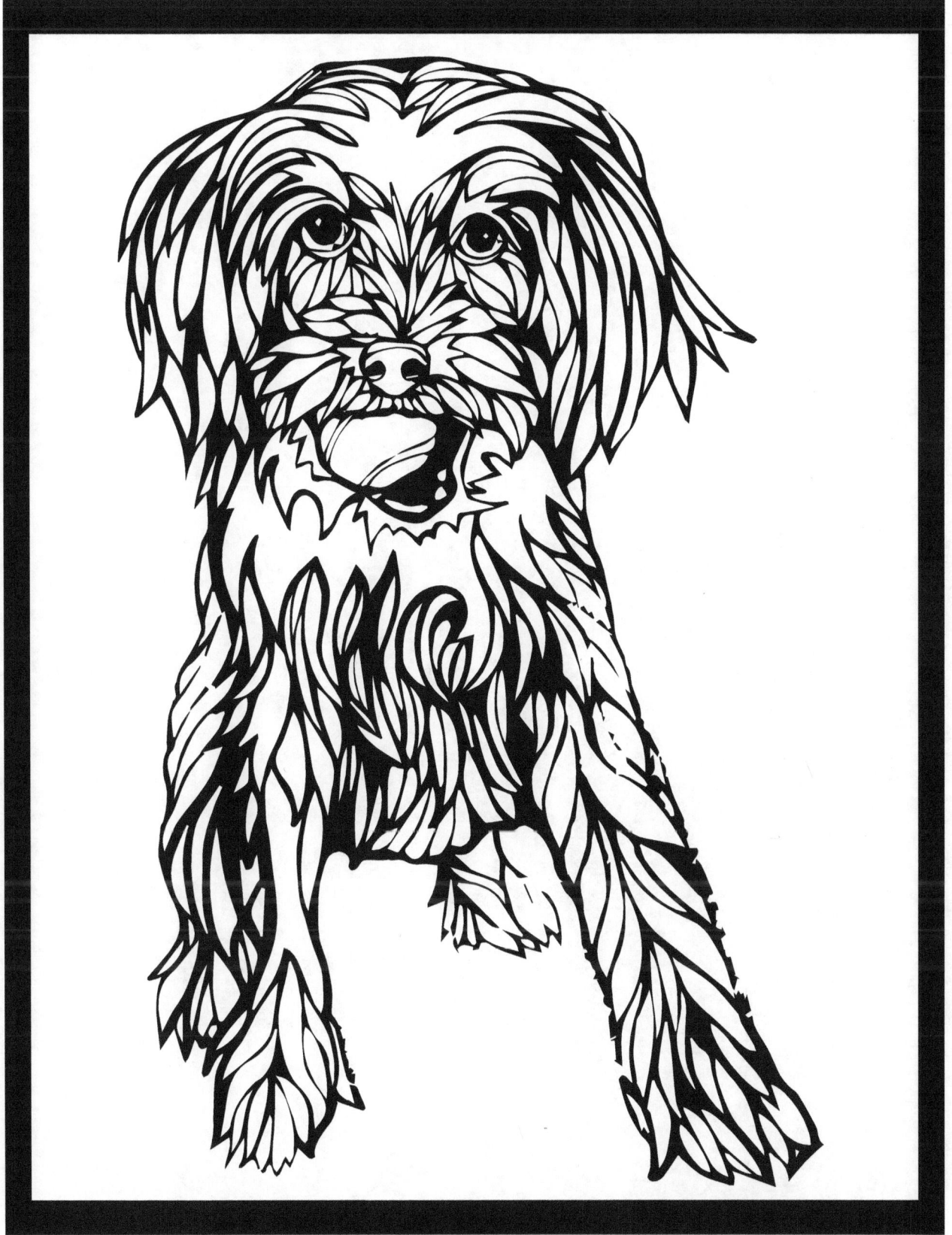

# SCOOTER

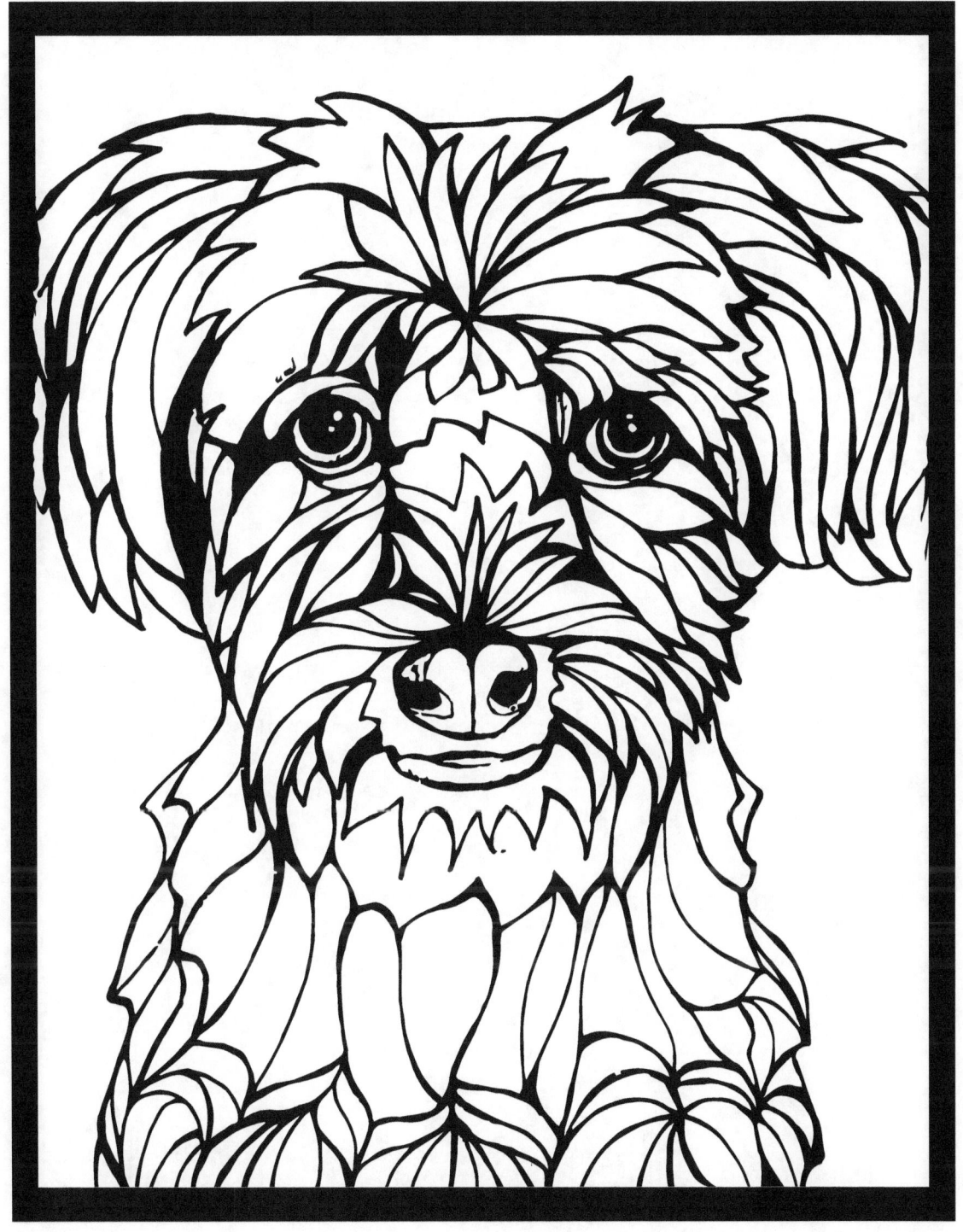

# SHRYNER

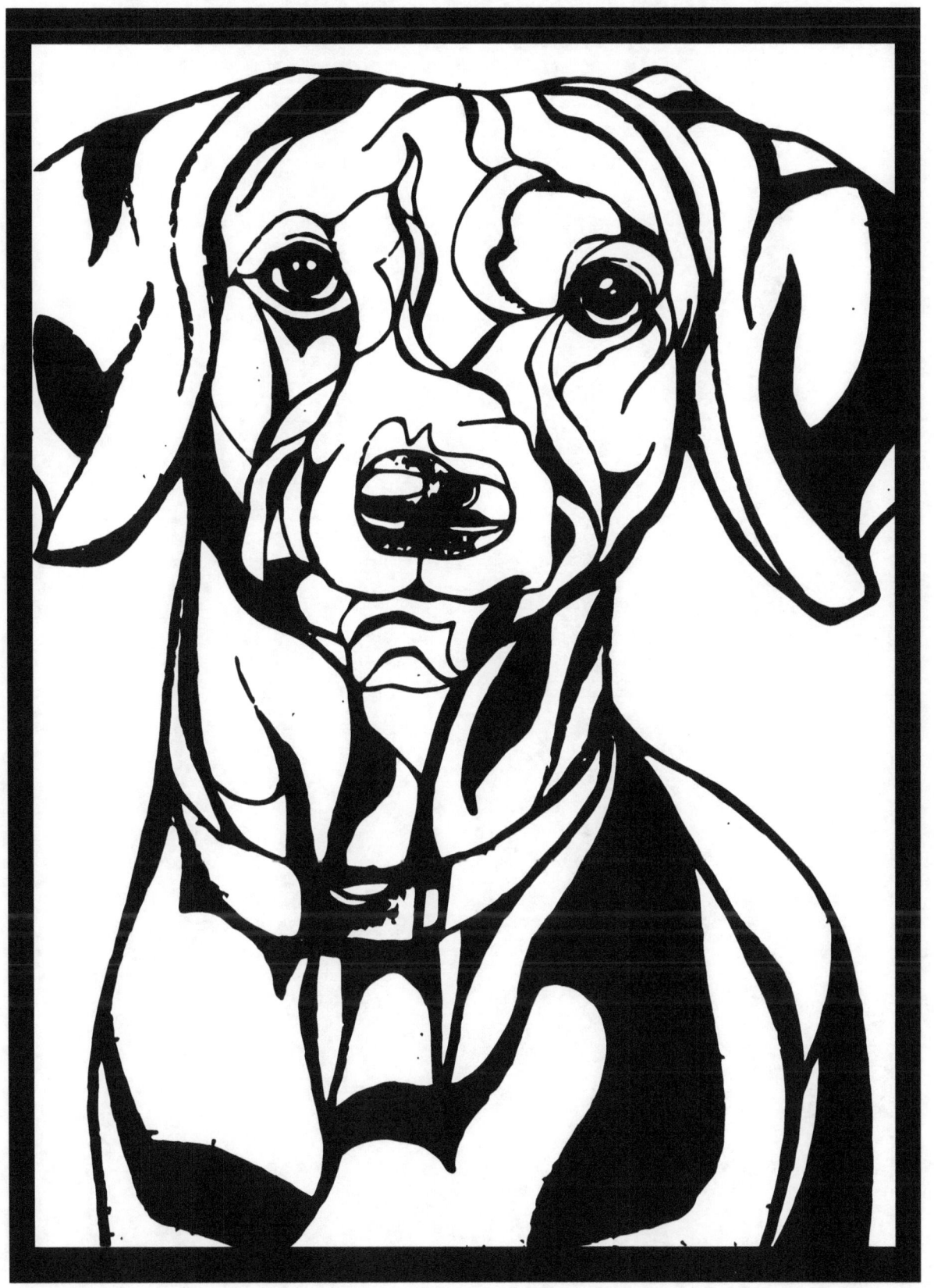

# SIRIUS

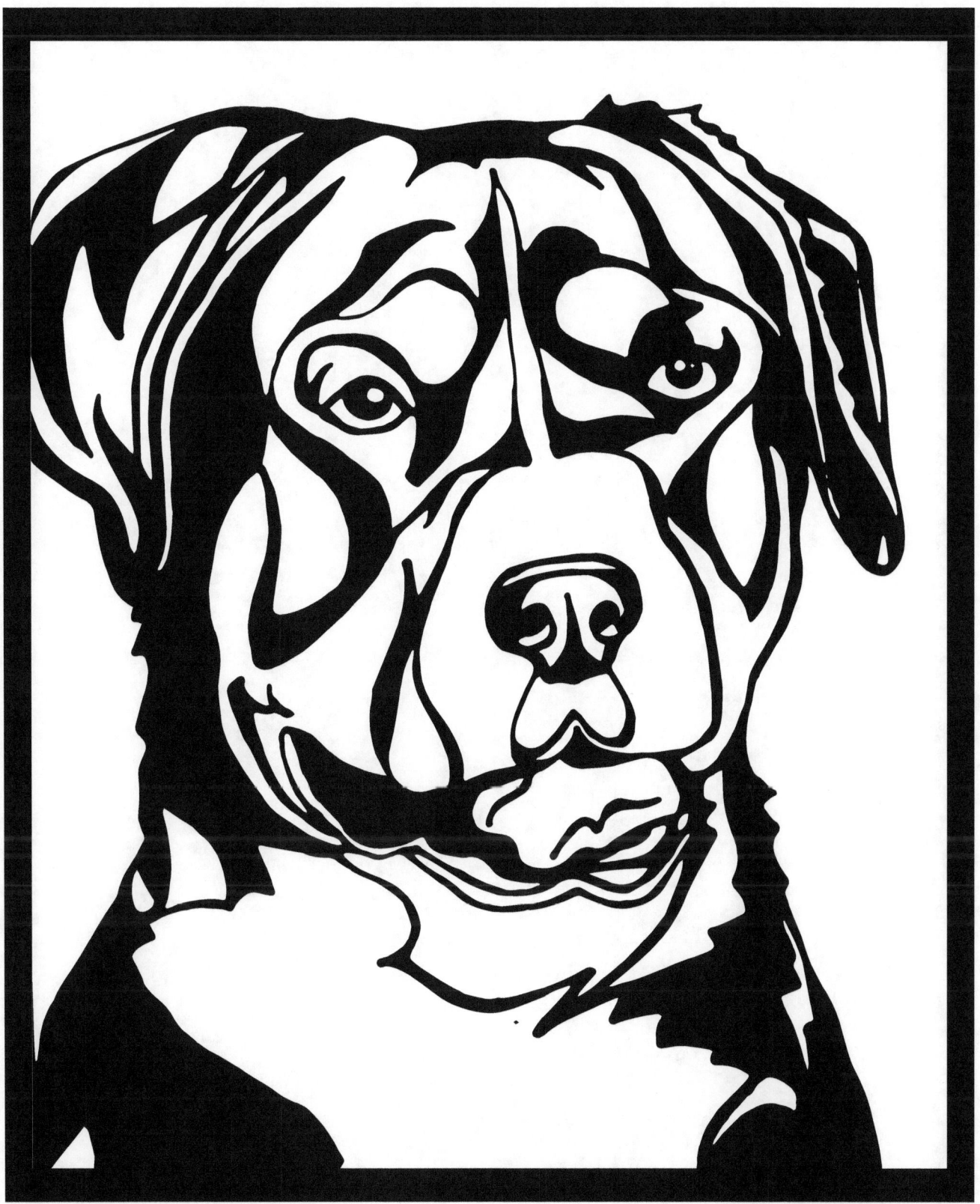

# STUCKY

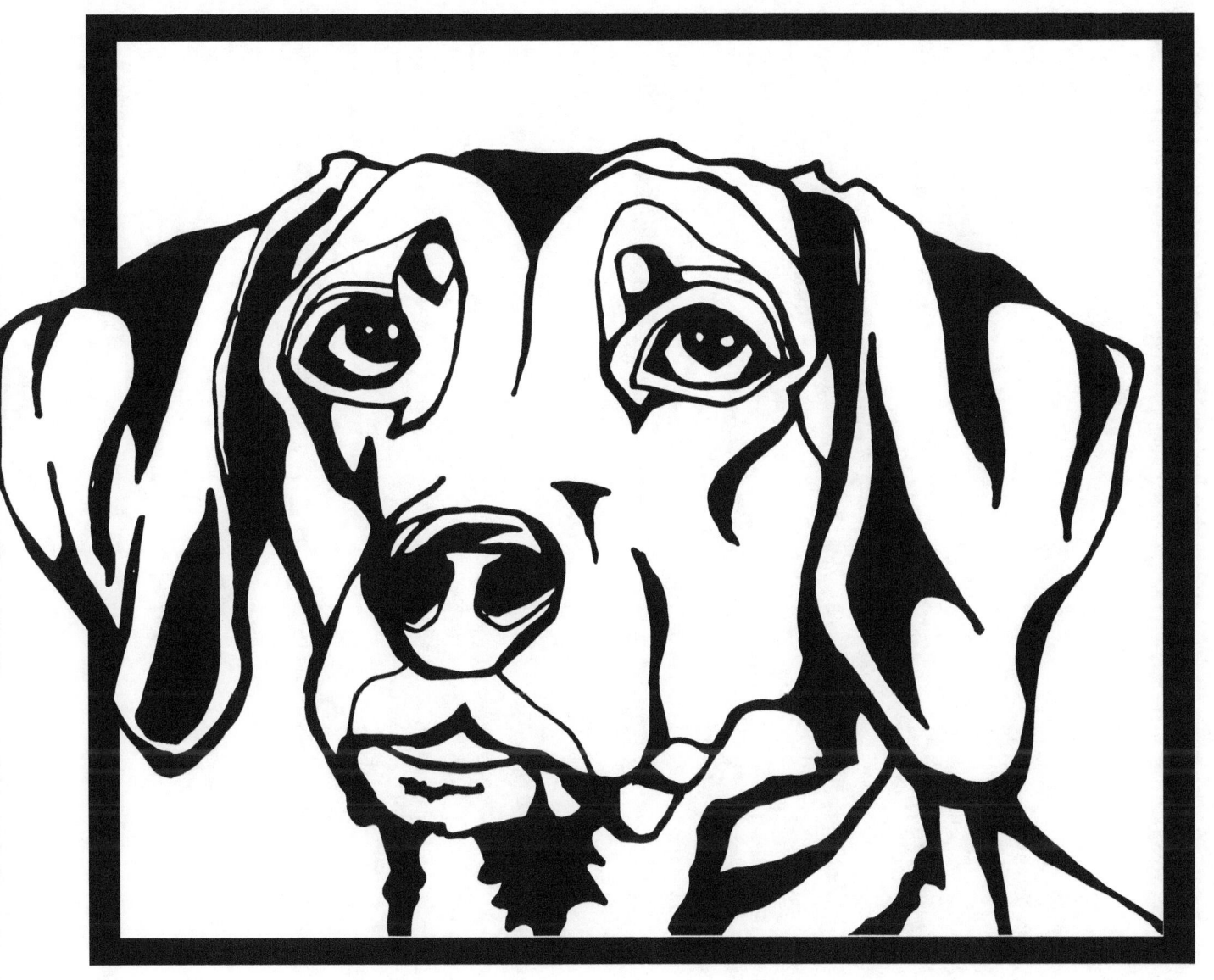

# SYLVAN

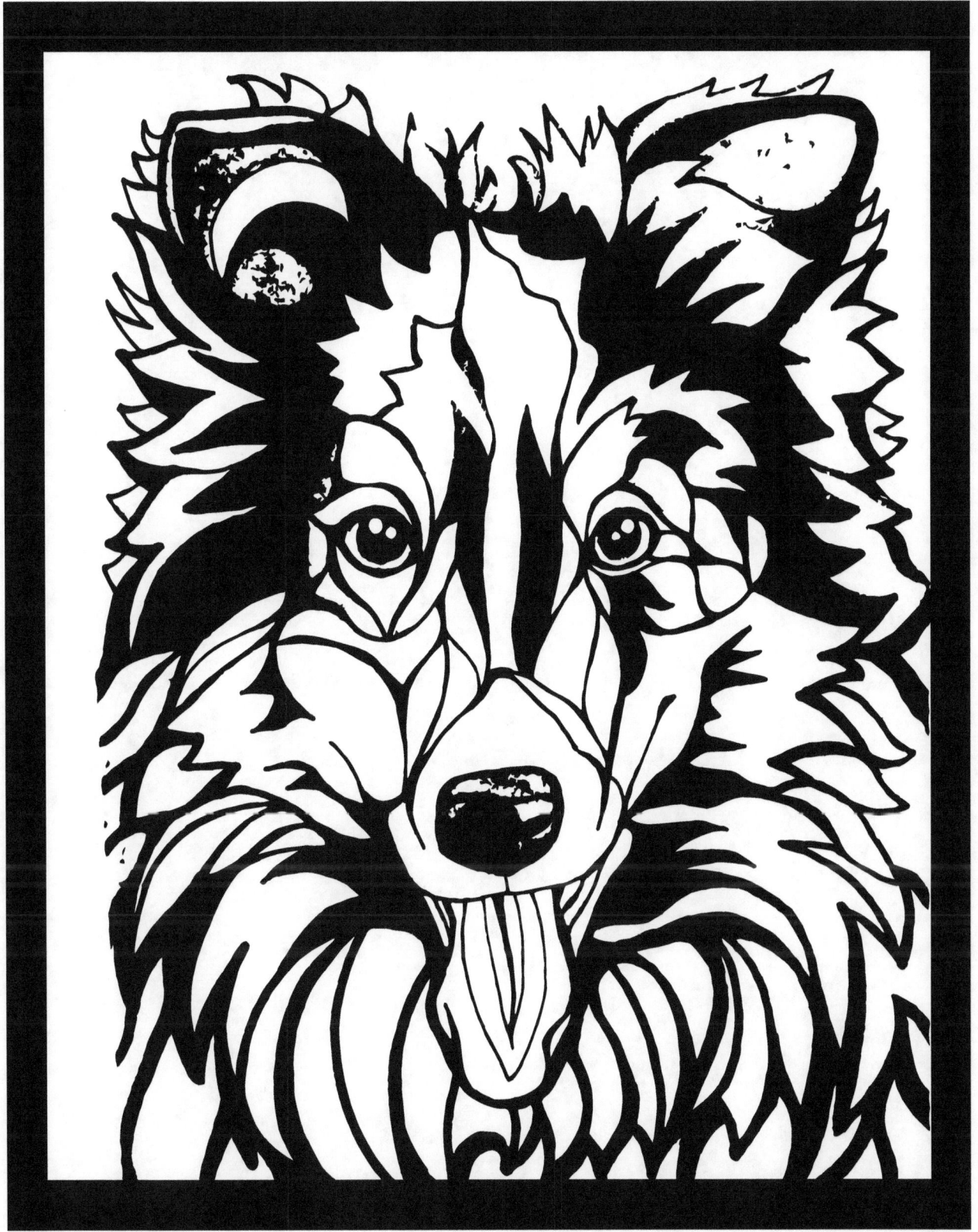

# TALULA

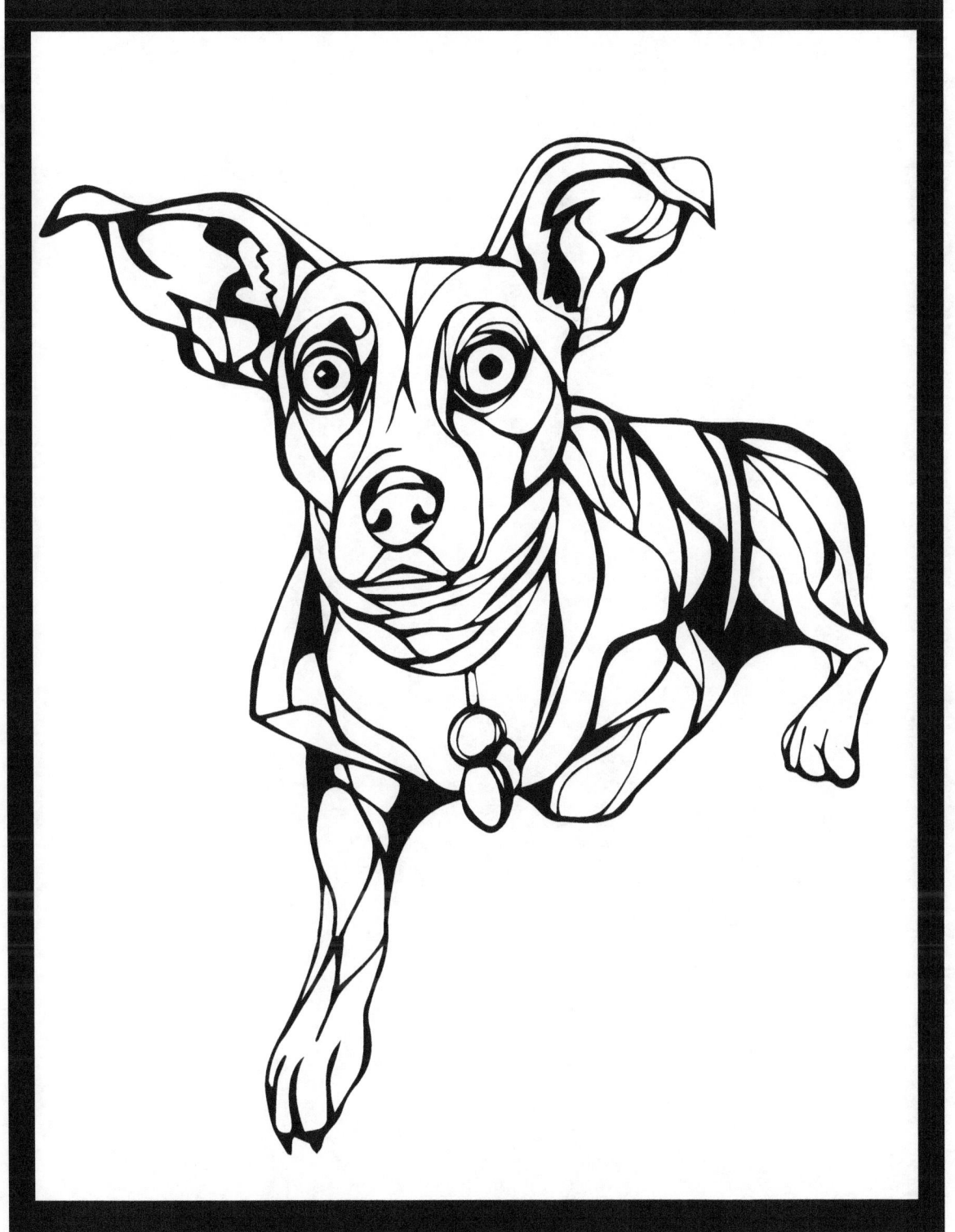

# TEDDY

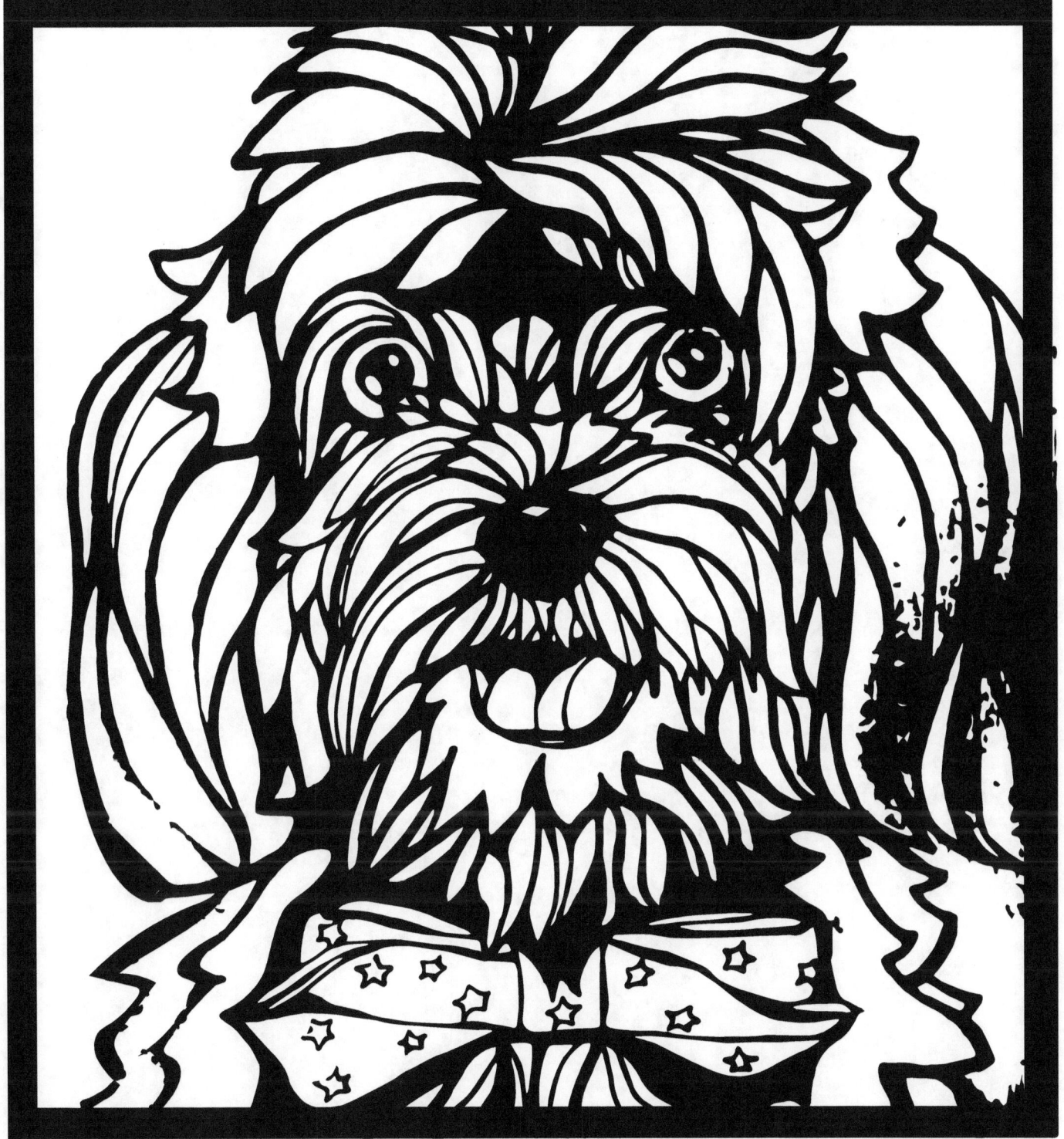

# WEISSWURST

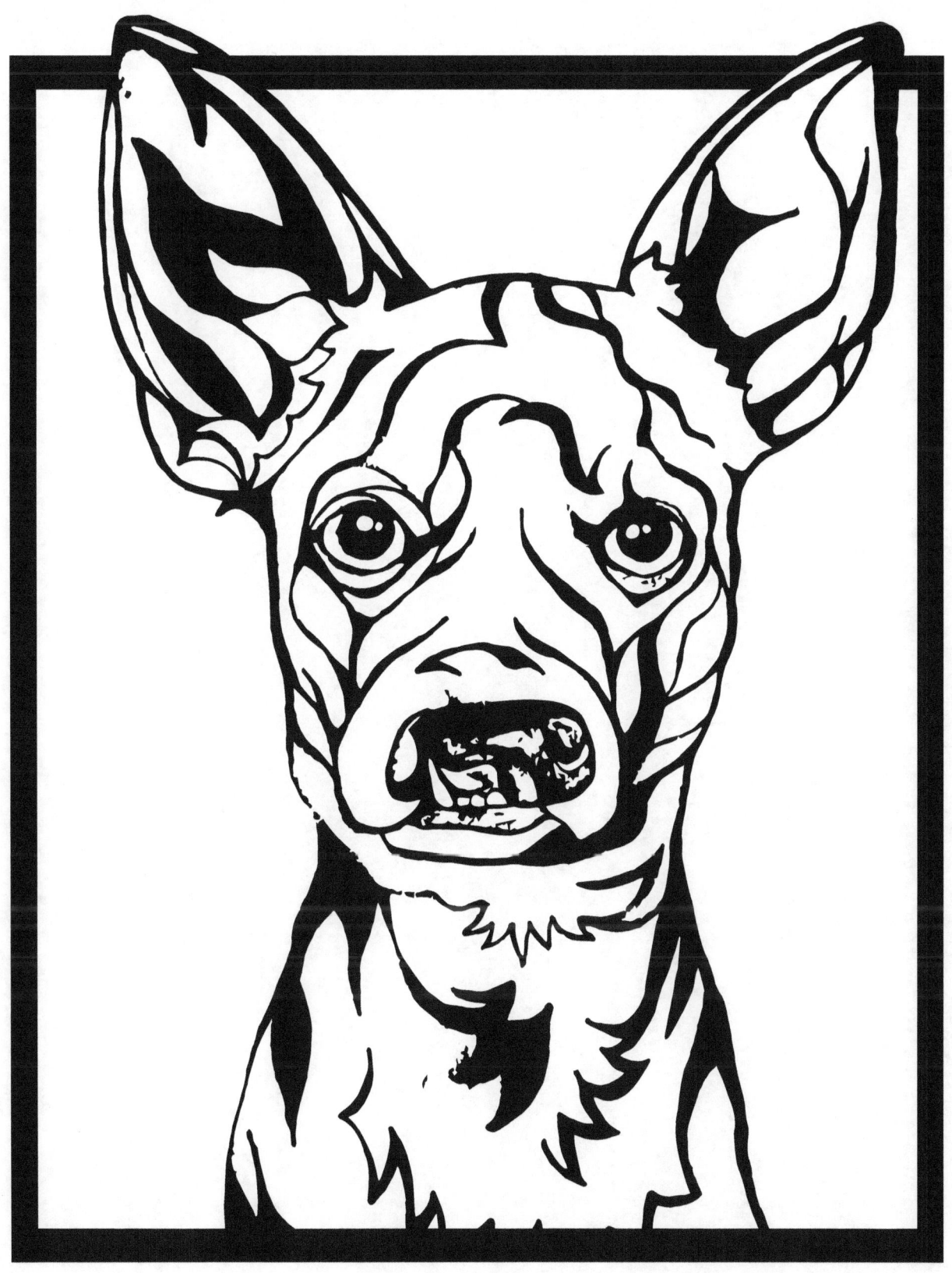

# WINSTON

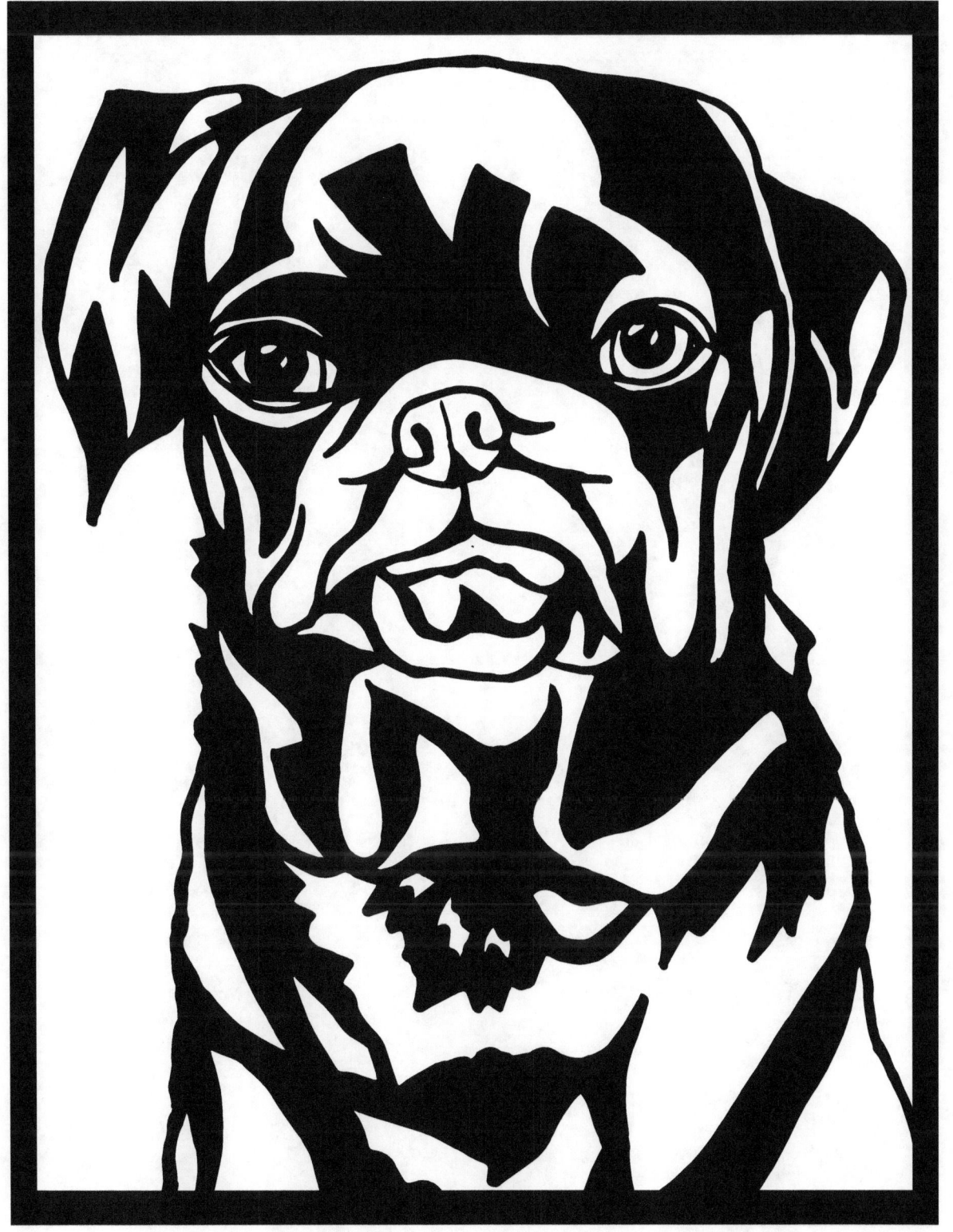

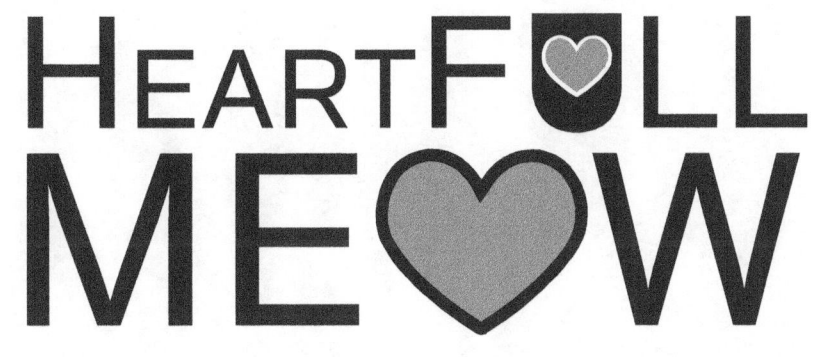

upcoming coloring book preview!

# JINXX

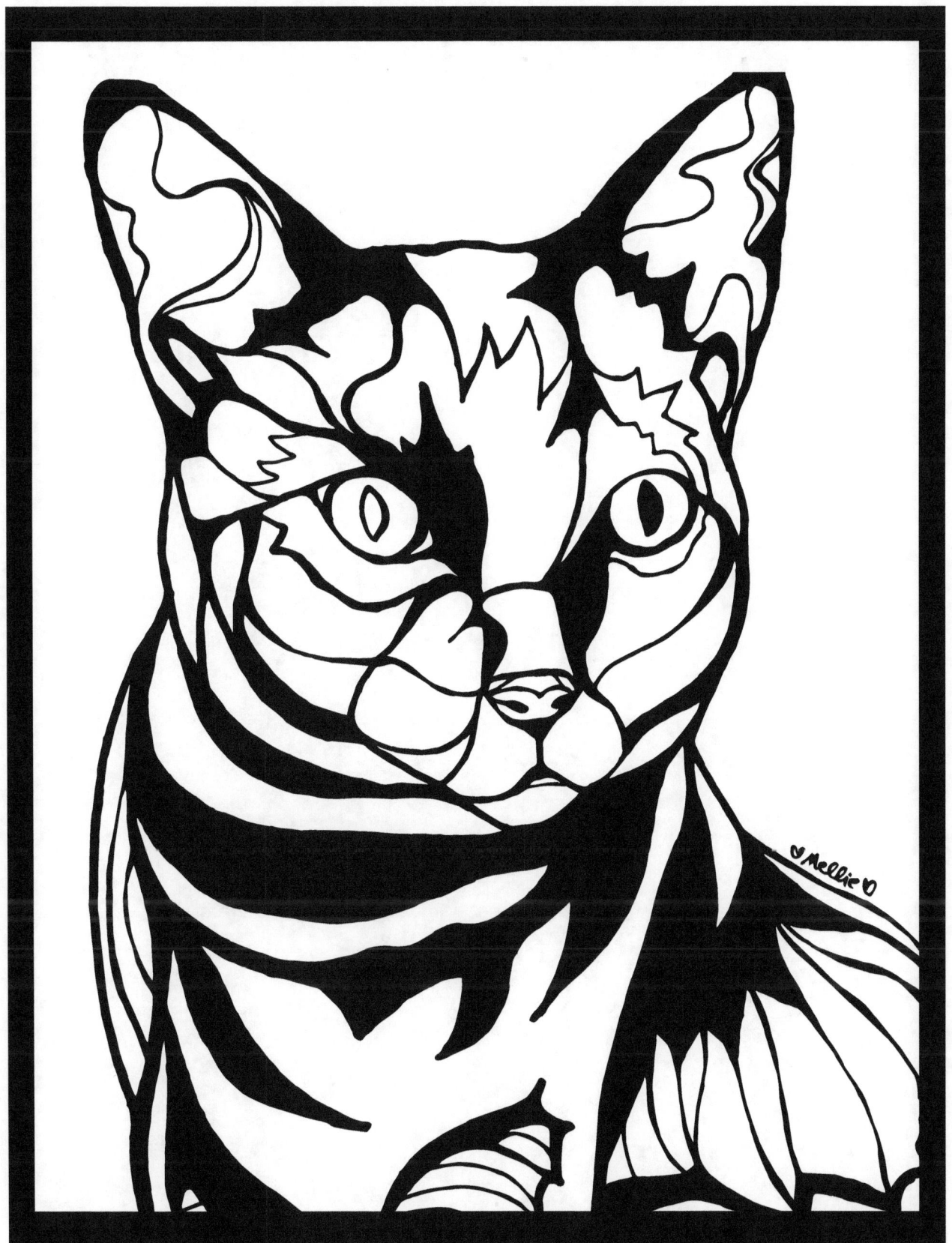

# GUSTAV

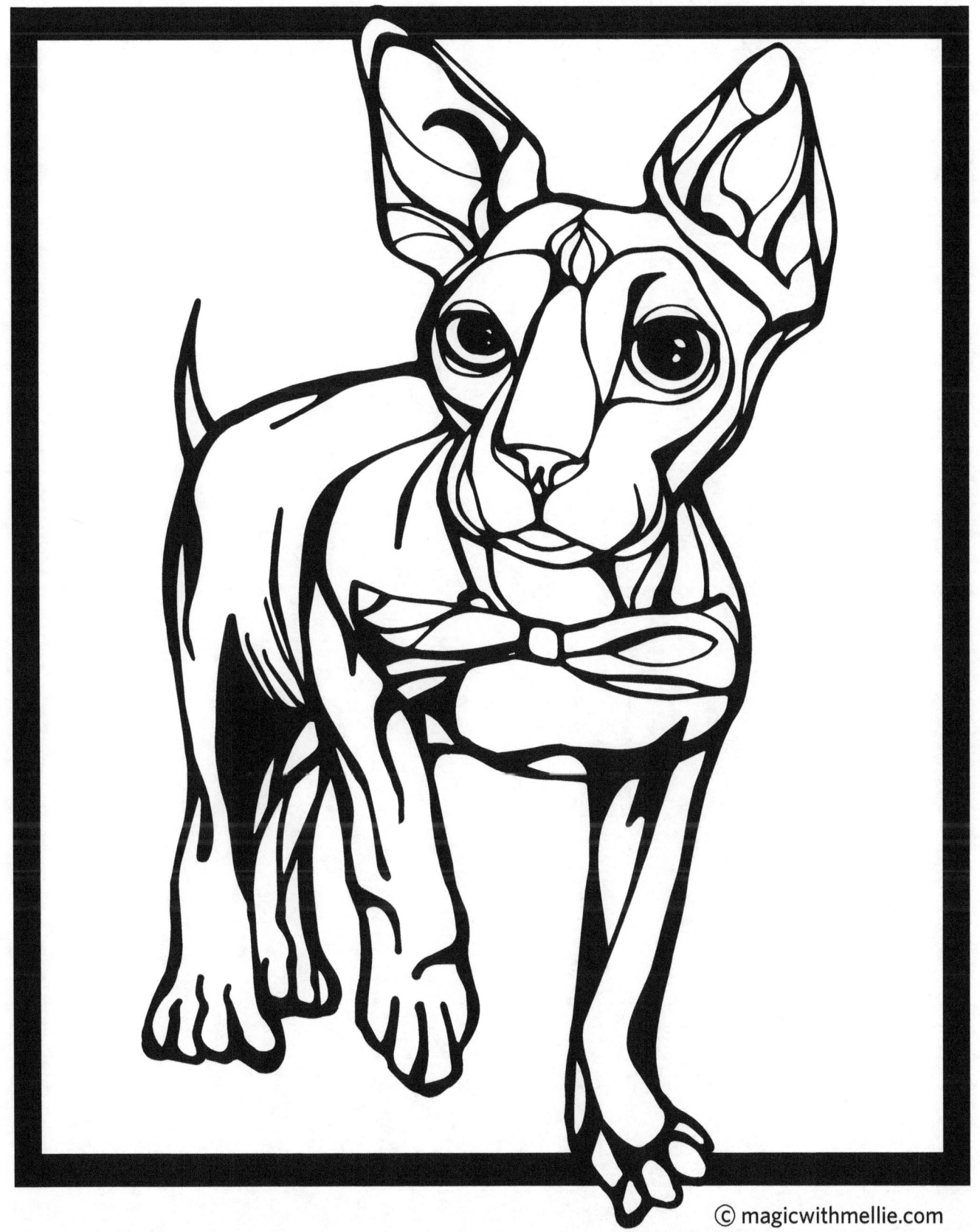

# HeartFULL HORSES

## upcoming coloring book preview!

# JOSEPH

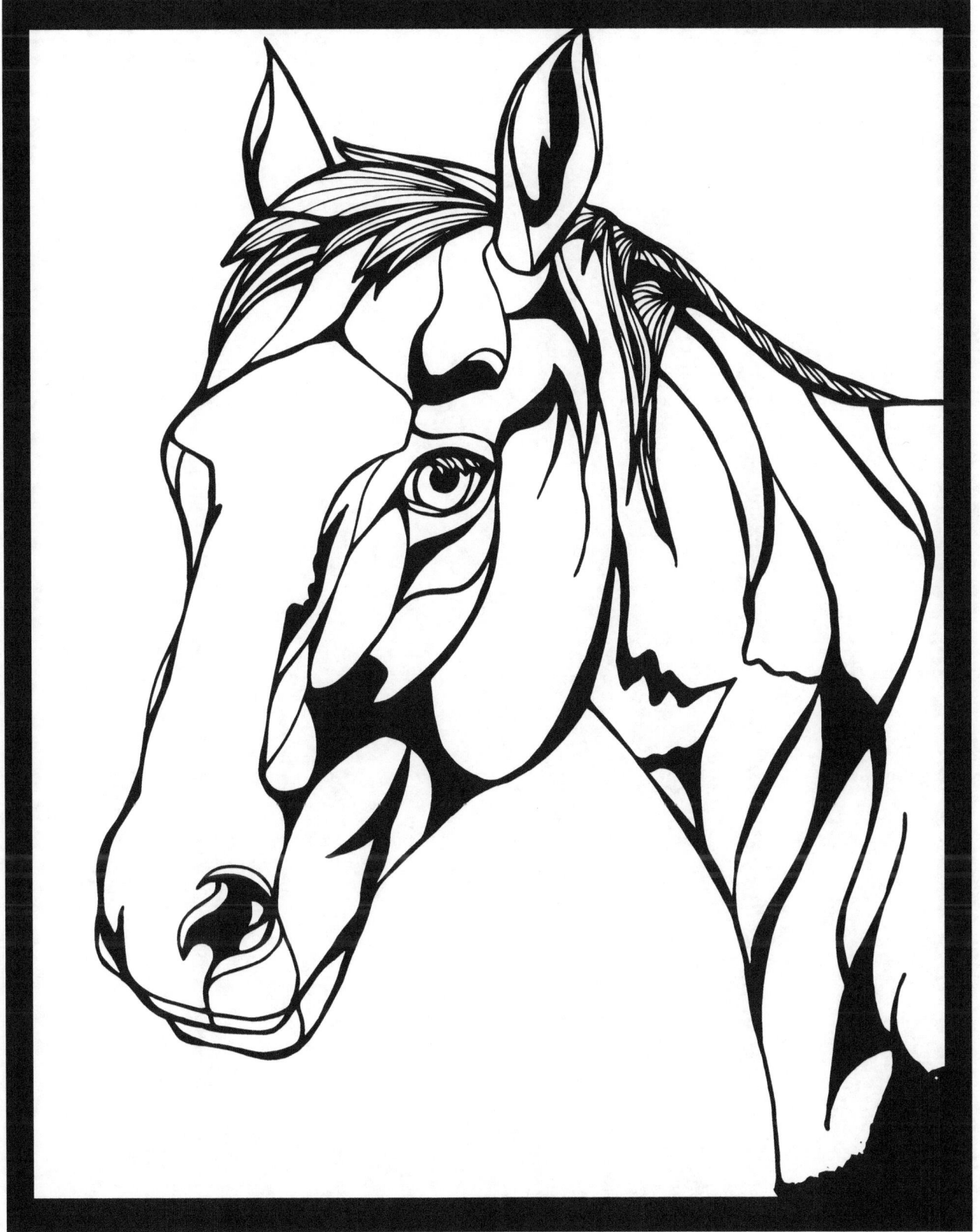

# SHADY

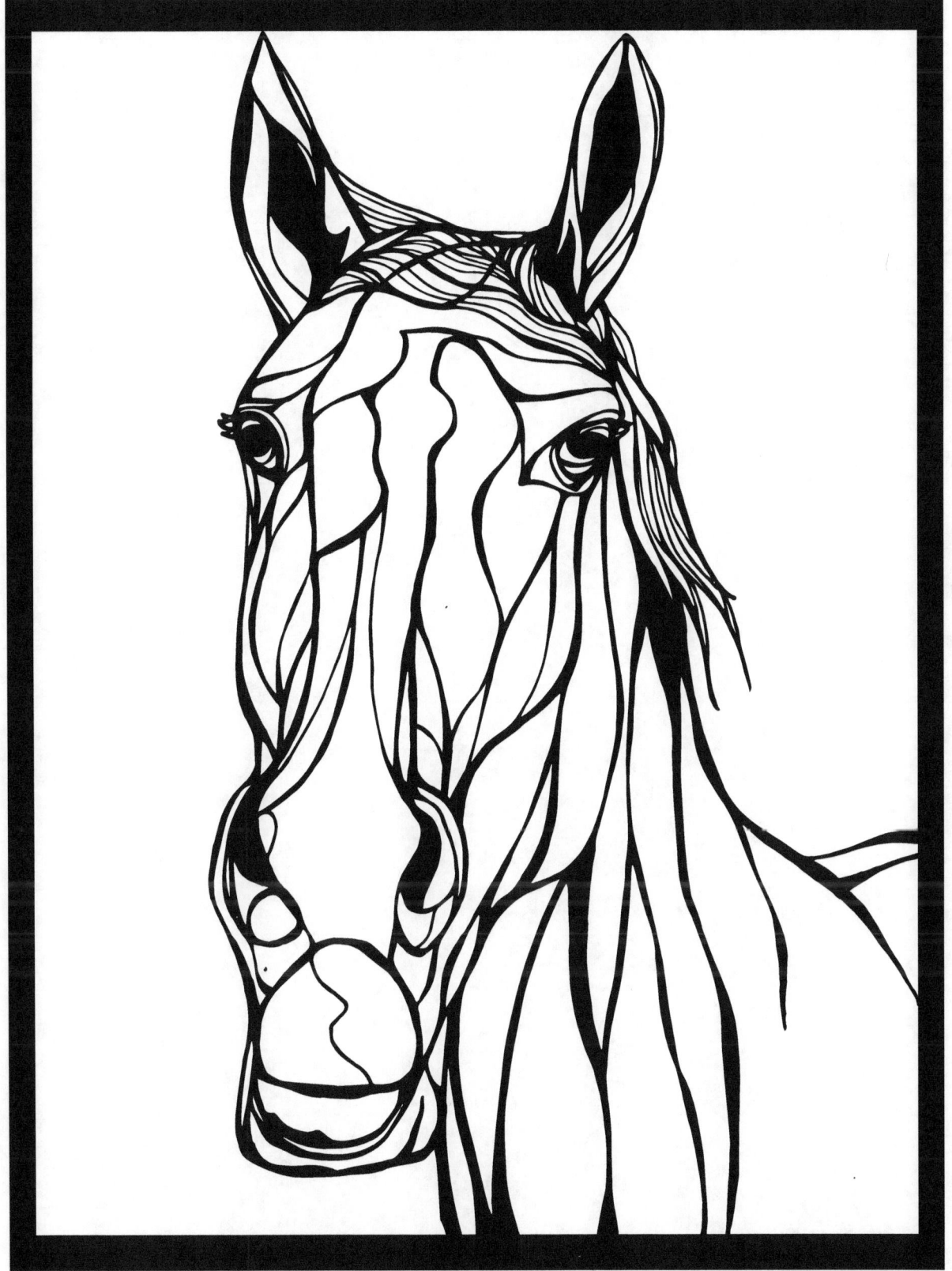

#  about the author/illustrator

Magical Melanie (Mellie) Test lives with her 7yo son and dogs in the mountains of Western Colorado. She's been creative and intuitive her entire life, but has only recently begun to claim the full power of her gifts.

Before migrating to colorful Colorado, Mellie lived in Northern Virginia (the Washington, D.C. area) for nearly 17 years, and has also lived in Kentucky, Nebraska (where she was born), Pennslvania (outside of Philly), Kansas, and Missouri. Colorado is by far her favorite, and the freedom she feels hiking to the top of the Colorado peaks can't be topped (pun intended)!

She's rejuvenated by nature (whether it's hiking, rock climbing, paddleboarding, learning how to ski, or soaking in the local natural hot springs), spending time with her son and animals, and meeting with her international soul tribe online.

When she's not drawing or painting or creating intuitive art lesson videos for her Daily Blog and free Facebook group (called "Inspired Intuitive Art and Action"), Mellie also supports her family through freelance graphic design projects and a "real job" role as a Sales Liaison and Ad Designer in Basalt, Colorado near Aspen.

# ♥ a fond farewell : stay in touch! ♥

I hope you had fun experiencing the MAGIC that each of these dogs — whether in form or in spirit — has offered to you through these enchanted dog portraits!

Please feel free to connect with me online. And if you feel drawn to the energy of my work, I would LOVE to create some magical original pet portrait art for you, too!

Website and Social:
    MagicWithMellie.com
    facebook.com/MagicWithMellie
    instagram.com/HeartFULLPets
    youtube.com/HeartFULLPets

Ordering Custom Pet Portraits:
    bit.do/HeartFULLPets

Prints and Products:
    bit.do/redbubblemellie

Messages from the Dogs Oracle Deck:
    bit.do/dogsoracledeck

My Animals of Inspiration Magically Infused Coloring Book:
    http://bit.do/animalsofinspiration

Or email Mellie@MagicWithMellie.com if you need more magic in your life!

www.ingramcontent.com/pod-product-compliance
Lightning Source LLC
Chambersburg PA
CBHW080715190526
45169CB00006B/2388